In the
Valley of Tears

In the Valley of Tears

Patrick Autréaux

Translated by Eduardo A. Febles

In the Valley of Tears **was** originally published as
Dans la vallée des larmes
ISBN 2070123889
© 2009 by Éditions Gallimard, Paris

Cover art: "Colony," Terry Winters, 1983

ISBN 978-1-942254-12-6
Library of Congress Control Number: 2019905481

Contents

Translator's note

I was forty-five years old when I was diagnosed with stage III colon cancer.

I had been told for a year that I was simply suffering from hemorrhoids. I finally asked my primary care doctor for further tests since I thought something else was wrong. He agreed to order a colonoscopy even though I did not fit the profile of typical colon cancer patients. The procedure took place on July 21st, 2016. I was still groggy, the effects of the mild anesthesia waning, when the doctor pronounced a certain word to the nurse, both looking at an image on the screen behind my back as I laid on my side, a word I prayed I had misheard. With surgical precision, he told the nurse: "This will have to come out." Anyone who has had the misfortune of hearing the "c" word knows how much of a shock it is, and how scary.

A new routine started for me and my husband, one of medical appointments, expectations, and hopes. A preliminary CT scan showed that the cancer had not metastasized and the surgeon was optimistic that surgery alone would get rid of the cancer. Much to my chagrin, I couldn't avoid chemotherapy, since, after the operation, we discovered that two lymph nodes had been compromised. A port was placed in my chest, and I followed a strict regimen of Folfox chemotherapy from October of 2016 to March of 2017, infused every two weeks. It was during those difficult months of chemotherapy that I found solace in the project of translating a French novel I had heard about five years earlier.

In fact, the weekend before my colonoscopy, I had contacted Patrick Autréaux for the very first time via e-mail. I was looking for a new project, and his voice had lingered in my memory for several years. In 2011, while on sabbatical in Paris, I had heard Autréaux speaking about his work *Dans la vallée des larmes* (2009) during an interview with Laure Adler for the France Culture radio show, *Hors-Champs*. The tone and cadence of his sentences pleased me as he answered frankly to the questions posed; the story of a psychiatrist suddenly finding himself "on the other side", the side of a cancer patient, was compelling. I made a mental note to myself: "I need to read his works." I didn't until that summer of 2016, before my diagnosis; little did I know then that I would find myself "on the other side" with him.

I took the fact that I had contacted Autréaux precisely the weekend before I was diagnosed as a sign of destiny: I had found the project that would help me mentally endure the physical treatments I was to undergo. Rather than wallowing in the situation at hand, I became an automaton, setting aside emotions and reveling in the intellectual process of comparing languages and the detective work of finding the right expressions to render Autréaux's words in English. In some ways, I had put a parenthesis around the illness to keep at bay those questions which Autréaux rightly tells us not to ask when confronted with calamities beyond our control: "If I let my thoughts go down that slippery slope, I would immediately land in a circle of hell more dreadful than the one I was already in."

Autréaux's importance in today's French literary landscape is indisputable. In a recent interview during the France Culture show *J'ai déjà connu le bonheur,* Jean-Christophe Rufin called him one of France's greatest living authors in terms of the quality of his work. Indeed, Autréaux has become an established author in France, having penned already six major works, which include his trilogy on illness, *Dans la vallée des larmes* (2009), *Soigner* (2010), and *Se survivre* (2013); a work of fiction, *Les irréguliers* (2015); an autobiographical essay, *La voix écrite* (2017); and a play for the Avignon Theater Festival, *Le grand vivant* (2015). He has also written short stories and critical essays on art, literature, politics, and mystical saints.

Autréaux was born in 1968 near Fontainebleau, south of Paris. He evokes some of his childhood memories in his autobiographical pieces, particularly in *Soigner*, describing the illness that eventually took his grand-mother away, his parents' troubled marriage and eventual divorce, and the love for his grand-father. As a young boy, he had already decided to become a doctor and a poet. In *Soigner*, he writes: "From what I've been told again and again, as a kid, I had already declared that I would become a doctor. One evening, after seeing *Doctor Zhivago* on TV, I added: and poet. Doctor and poet." He began with the first one to later become the second. A brilliant medical student, he pursued psychiatry and eventually became an ER doctor so as to have the flexibility to travel between France and the United States, where his partner was living. Just before turning 35, however, his life suddenly changed: while visiting Chicago, he was diagnosed with the same cancer that afflicted his grand-mother. The prognosis was rather grim; he believed he had at most six months to live.

His trilogy on cancer was born in the midst of the despair stemming from an imminent death. He describes with acuity a paradoxical vision of ultimate solitude accompanied by extreme serenity: "I floated over a void of fullness and inexistence. I was still alive, whole—entirely whole, not in pieces—but I was no longer at the center of my being. . . . I felt haunted by an unnamable internal unity cutting me off from everything around me. I was unbelievably untouched." *Coup de théâtre*, once back in

France, he received a different prognosis, and the possibility of a treatment which, albeit difficult, could lead to a remission of the cancer. Autréaux describes laconically the grueling side-effects of chemotherapy: "As the effects of the treatments compounded, I withered and floated away toward a no-man's-land." After his recovery, he tried to go back to work as a doctor, yet, something had changed. The experience of the illness cast a different light upon his patients, he was no longer able to find the necessary aloofness required to treat others. He thus abandoned medical practice to dedicate himself solely to letters.

Though at the surface this might seem like an abrupt about-face, on the contrary, Autréaux finds a seamless continuity between the doctor's goals of healing patients and the mission of literature as ultimate repository of human hopes and aspirations. A sort of religious experience—the title *Dans la vallée des larmes* comes from a biblical verse (Psalm 84:6)—literature allows the writer to reach out and help his or her reader. In the interview cited above with Laure Adler, he explains that "Fulfilling myself through writing and literature is a better way of being able to help others fulfill themselves." He learns this particular lesson from his readings while ill, especially from Primo Levi's writings about the Holocaust. In fact, he sets up in *Dans la vallée de larmes* a taxonomy of literary works: on the one hand, the generous, life-affirming ones exemplified by Primo Levi; on the other hand, works that lead through hopelessness to despair, such as Fritz Zorn's *Mars*: "The two authors . . . played an almost Manichaean role during my long haul as a patient. Primo Levi, the moralist steamboat, guided and helped me return to my humanity; he conquered internal storms and saved me from spiritual shipwreck. Fritz Zorn's despair isolated me and cast me off to my fate; he threw me into a well of insurmountable solipsism, smashing against the absurdity of Evil." Autréaux's works clearly stand with the former.

I really did not know what I was signing up for when I decided to translate Autréaux's text. In my optimistic outlook—or perhaps I should call it naïveté—I believed I could finish the project rather quickly. The volume, after all, seemed rather slim at around 100 pages. Autréaux's style has been classified as classic, to which I would add extremely precise. His sentences can fluctuate from extremely laconic to fancifully lyrical. Therein lies one of the challenges of the project. However, I was doubly fortunate. First, I was able to meet Autréaux several times during the translation process since he lives in Boston part-time. Whenever I had a doubt about the meaning of a passage or word in a context, I could reach out to the living author for explanations, a luxury many translators do not have. And then, we were lucky enough to find Dr. Jonathan House, General Editor of The Unconscious in Translation. House took an early interest in our project and agreed to publish my translation, taking several risks: this was my first translation, Autréaux's book had not been translated into English before, and House specialized in psychoanalytic rather than literary titles. The coincidences, however, kept on flourishing: House has published a translation of Pontalis's *Frère du précédent* (*Brother of the Above*, translated by Donald Nicholson-Smith); Pontalis happens to be the original editor of *Dans la vallée des larmes* and continued to be Autréaux's editor until his death in 2013. House's encyclopedic knowledge of words in both languages brought interesting conversations and debates about the "correct" translation. His input was invaluable.

I have learned many lessons from my first translation, but I would like to highlight three of them here. While on chemotherapy, I was forced to think about my body constantly and in ways I had never done so before. My physical being took precedence and any symptom had to be recorded as possibly dangerous. That said, I did discover that the body is ultimately syntactic and therefore, always already a translation. As Autréaux points out in his *récit*, "I loved studying medicine; I was a passionate student: the double helix of DNA, the mosaic tiling of cells, the miniature rigging of transmitting networks and pipework filling us with life, the mechanics of lipid canals structuring tiny clocks as tiny as the speck on a speck of dust, the dance of proteins whose deficiency provokes calamities. Later, after the basic sciences, I loved the complex grammar of signs we learned to parse out on sick bodies." Contrary to Sontag's wish of releasing illness from metaphoric renderings, we apprehend the body through mental images that project upon it "a complex grammar of signs": illness is bad grammar. I also learned that translating is a communal experience. The stereotype of a translator alone at his or her desk with his or her tools at hand working in solitude do not reflect the reality of my experience. Quite the contrary, I felt myself in constant negotiations of meaning, elucidating not only the original in new ways, but creating a work of art in its own right. I hope to have done justice to the poetic and elegant style of Autréaux. And finally, I learned that suffering is translatable. Though we live in moments of great anxiety—in which groups tend to retreat into insular positions and solipsism reigns rampant—translating shows us that we can actually bridge beyond our limited lives and understand other cultures, other experiences, other ways of being. Ultimately, and to borrow Autréaux's own words, literature—and I would add, by extension, translation—allows the sharing of experiences that otherwise would not have come together.

Translator's Note

Cancer has become commonplace. The epidemic has cast a vast net, and you would be hard pressed to find someone who has not been touched by it. I feel fortunate to have been in remission for two years now. Others I know were not so lucky: my mother, María Vega de Febles, taken away by glioblastoma, my husband's mother, Carol Bean, and his father, Gary Ransom; one of my best friends during graduate studies at Brown University, Jacinta Wright, who succumbed to breast cancer.

To all of those battling this disease—or any disease, for that matter—I hope that you find in Autréaux's *In the Valley of Tears* a hand outstretched to help you find peace and strength. I certainly did.

Acknowledgments

As stated above, a translation project is not a solitary enterprise, but rather a communal experience at many levels—linguistic, historical, aesthetic, and cooperative. I'm grateful to Simmons University for its constant support throughout my career and illness. This project would not have come to fruition without a generous sabbatical granted in the Fall of 2017. I also want to thank the French government for a Hemingway grant awarded to this translation. I have been blessed with great colleagues at Simmons University and especially in the Department of Modern Languages and Literatures. They tirelessly support my endeavors. I thank all of them, too many to mention by name, but I hope they know who they are. My family has always encouraged me to cultivate the mind: I follow in the example of my parents who instilled a love and thirst for knowledge in me. I thank Jonathan House for taking a chance on me. I could not have asked for a better editor during this project. And of course, to Patrick: you were a beacon of hope during my season in hell. Thanks for producing such a beautiful text. *Merci*!

A special thanks to my husband Steven Ransom. He has been my unfaltering traveling companion throughout this funny thing called life, standing by my side in good and bad. It's difficult to translate into words how much I love you.

In the valley of sorrow, spread your wings.
— Susan Sontag

In the
Valley of Tears

I

I was just about to turn thirty-five when I was diagnosed with cancer.

I had been suffering from periodic stomachaches for several months. The doctors had ordered multiple tests, yet treatment had been to no avail. They blamed my life-style, my diet, my demanding job, and I accepted these explanations without being entirely convinced. I didn't dare imagine that something was devouring my gut.

After several days without pain, one evening a particularly agonizing episode sent me to the ER. I held my belly like a pregnant animal unsure of how to accomplish a difficult birth. Despite the crowd that evening, I was seen immediately.

It was the beginning of summer. A heat wave was in the air; the humidity weighed upon us; it felt as if the world were about to hatch. They took me toward a large area—the future, perhaps? A place in which moving forward would be difficult. There were gurneys everywhere, elderly patients panting in the hallways, nurses covering bodies, some people fanning themselves while moaning, and others griping because the air conditioning wasn't working.

I don't clearly remember the hours that followed. We remain in a way outside ourselves at the moment of our birth. Especially when, at the same time, we realize we are condemned.

I was placed in a cubicle, and through the half-open door, I could hear someone describing a grim case. A resident came in to alert me that my scans revealed bad news. The young man uttered a few words amounting to my death sentence. Light passed through me, hitting me as if I were trapped inside a crystal ball. My vision was at once blinded and infinitely clear-sighted.

Resigned to wait on my gurney, I gave up all hope. I knew.

After several hours, they transferred me to another department, to another room, and settled me inside the railings of a bright white bed. Like never before, a hospital appeared like a gate upon which is written: *"Lasciate ogne speranza, voi ch'entrate."* Abandon all hope, ye who enter here. I drifted away.

Lying in the dark, I was in a state of shock. The pain had subsided with the morphine. I might have slept a bit. My mind merged with the room, and until dawn, I couldn't differentiate darkness from sleep, nor from myself. That is what death must be like.

A surgeon paid me a visit very early the next morning, accompanied by the resident from the night before, who seemed tired, and by some externs with gloomy faces. I was no longer on the same side of life as they were. Something dangerous and ambiguous weighed down the room, a weird and inevitable truth, like looking at your hand and being surprised to find five fingers on it. Only the strangeness of everything remained.

The surgeon was a big guy, a rugby-player type. He wore the grave and troubled expression doctors use in circumstances such as this.

He's standing in front of the bed. I cannot straighten up. He sees me wincing and introduces himself.

"You know why we kept you here, right?"

Yes, but could he explain it again?

"A tumor has practically invaded all of your intestines. There is a risk of serious hemorrhage. We shouldn't delay the surgery."

What is it, exactly? He utters words I cannot hear.

It is dead silent around him, and the light seems to dim once again, as if mourning. He asks whether the medical students can examine me. They don't seem to feel a thing. The resident explains to them how to do it, but the surgeon cuts the lesson short. I ask why I didn't feel any pain before. It was spread thinly enough, he says, to fool even many clinicians. It's also hard to fathom oneself being sick, right?

To conclude, he shakes my hand with a "good luck." I don't answer. I don't cry. He has uttered the name of an incurable cancer. A death sentence.

For two weeks, until a precise diagnosis could be established, I remained convinced I was condemned and, at best, had six months to live.

I couldn't imagine what would come next, except that I was going to suffer horribly. They had treated me with tranquilizers, and the surgeon had promised the surgery would relieve all symptoms. I needed to believe what he said. I sank into my bed, watching the bare wall in front of me, the drops from the IV falling like cold seconds. Suddenly, everything was eclipsed; fearful thoughts of chaos and suffering slipped away. I was in a cradle or bassinet, swaddled by death. I was terrified and yet no longer afraid. At its heart, violence is calm. I think I lifted the sheets to look at my body, maybe to say good-bye to myself. My stomach looked funny, my penis too, as if lack of desire had shrunken it to almost nothing. My body had betrayed me and let an unknown enemy invade me. Facing hostile fire, I retreated inside my head. When great sorrow arises, one is but a mere snail.

People passed near the room without entering. I had the impression they were avoiding it. A muffled resonance came from monitors, from faraway voices and footsteps, from the sounds of phones ringing, a little as after an explosion, there remains in the ear and in the body paralyzed by the shock a deaf sound that is neither sound nor vibration but the imprint of the shock.

I floated over a void of fullness and inexistence. I was still alive, whole—entirely whole, not in pieces—but I was no longer at the center of my being; instead, there was a vacuum full of something without sensory content; a light without light; a presence without body; a consciousness without memory, without emotion. I felt haunted by an unnamable internal unity cutting me off from everything around me. I was unbelievably untouched.

My partner, Benjamin, immediately decided to come back to Paris to care for me as long as necessary.

We had met about ten years before, when he was finishing up his studies in France. Soon after, he accepted a university position in New York. I had chosen to remain and practice in an emergency department, which allowed me a flexible schedule so I could visit him frequently. We led a transatlantic life.

When he knocked on the door of my hospital room, doctors were examining me for the umpteenth time. A nurse asked him to wait. From the doorway his eyes searched for mine. The room closed in on his troubled expression. A great sorrow seized me, for him, for us. Benjamin couldn't do a thing.

Everything was happening too fast. Once you've crossed to the other side of life, you must undress at command, accept the discomforts and restrictions of medical protocols. You need to manage as best you can, find a way to make sense of it all, find something to hold on to. That's why doctors are hated. They reveal the unexpected, sever your bonds, and leave you in pieces without being able to guide you, without really caring about having opened the door to solitude and the absolute.

After a short respite, anxiety quickly returned due to the surgeon's frankness. Upon reflecting on what was happening to me and where it could lead, I felt as if I could not breathe. I had to avoid that vertiginous slope where there was no joy, only fear, and to surrender to the doctors. Even if, after putting myself in their hands, I retreated into a state of uncertainty, my uncertainty echoing and multiplying theirs, undermining the internal clarity I had experienced in bed during the first morning. I conjured it up again to save me: They were taking care of me, but also bringing me back to the land of fear where appeasement vanished—the appeasement found in empty plenitude, in that me without me, in the invulnerability that had led me to experience that particular *vision*.

I couldn't imagine that setting out on the long path toward a cure also meant undertaking a much longer journey—not back to my previous life, but rather toward accepting a heart both dreadful and soothing shining and beating within me, a heart that I felt when they let me understand that I was a lost case.

It was the starting line of a long road across a land in which words had been emptied out and silenced by a terrible salvo. Only a shell without meaning remained, language shaking words the way the wind shakes muted rattles. Or rather, words meant something so deathly absolute, by their very emptiness, that they lost their proper sense. Slowly they came back to life, but before they inhabited their shells again, this sense of being outside of language would remain the only sign capable of meaning something. It was obvious. I was nothing but a living sign.

Most of the time, being a doctor affords you the advantage of not fearing what is worrisome to others. You are less sensitive to the minor fears arising from hospital rituals; you can clearly see reassuring details, even if you are terrorized by what others ignore or cannot imagine. While to others it is shrouded in mystery, you know the health care system so well that it manifests itself with remarkable transparency.

X-ray exams. One step among others.

Nurses and hospital attendants walk around, chit-chatting in the hallways. The nurses' aides joke among themselves. A young girl waits wrapped in a sheet, tube in her nose, eyes fixed on nothing. A bed carrying a comatose patient hooked up to tubes bangs against the doors. A gentleman in pajamas, urine bag between his legs, reads the newspaper next to a white-haired lady.

Consciousness is the only wealth we possess; it expands, and its kingdom opens deeper into the invisible. You can see an amorphous thing floating in drafts between people's legs, searching for its place, weaving in and out of the labyrinth formed by seats and armchairs, before settling in dusty corners. Someone shouts, "Close the door, for crying out loud!" Three women, elbows resting on the reception desk, don't budge.

Pushed by a stranger, I leave the waiting room. Nothing ahead but suspense. After a ritual of questions, IVs, potions to drink—all of which will remain more or less the same in the checkups in the years to come—the giant ring of the CAT scan finally slides above. The truth serum has been injected. Waves of heat arise from the iodine. On the monitor, the Evil will appear and take on the aspect of an impending storm waiting to burst. Later, while examining the images from the scan, we will contemplate the storm. But for now, only imminent knowledge matters: You can no longer hold on to anything, neither curiosity, nor annoyance, nor surprise at the behavior of people at the hospital. Pure panic sets in—a purity without purpose, like those minerals that have killed everything in them, becoming transparent, unchanging. A panic that strips you so completely naked that compassion, kindness, and the need for affection disappear. You don't even try to dodge bullets anymore.

You emerge from the scanner. The kind women discussing their winter vacation plans help you down from the motorized table and place you in a wheelchair. Outside of the room, you watch the hospital attendants pass by, and you wait for the one who will call out your name. Suddenly, you feel a great need for a loving presence.

Every time I thought of Benjamin during those two weeks I believed I was condemned—I suffered as if it were he that was dead. I couldn't bring myself to imagine that I would not live long enough to see the winter.

I had surgery. The prognosis was better than expected. There was even talk of being cured.

Months of chemotherapy followed. The doctors worked hard on the cancer while I was drifting. My time was split between the day hospital and my bed. As the effects of the treatments compounded, I withered and floated away toward a no-man's-land.

Considerate and infinitely cautious, Benjamin remained in Paris throughout my treatment. Together we had faced some difficult times, some caused by our families and some due to painful losses, so we had become each other's family. This was the first time he'd had to confront such a tough situation alone.

Now and then, I had to be rushed to the ER. Benjamin would accompany me, attempting to hide any signs of worry; but how could you miss his washed-out face? He kept to himself what the nurses said behind closed doors, what he heard or read about the illness and treatments and their long-term effects. He saw my limbs melting away, my skin ulcerating, fevers wiping me out. He would prop me up with cushions and cook up small meals so that I'd gain some weight. He searched for solutions to the chemo's side effects, which the doctors did not really want to hear about.

When a word becomes reality, that which seemed bearable becomes as tormenting as a vulture. As soon as you feel the onset of side effects, they feast on you like hyenas devouring your entrails. Is that why you are so preoccupied with them, these, the strangest of foreigners in oneself? The symptoms of illness are shrouded in a mysterious aura, arising from a depth that one fears and listens to: They are fate's toxic effusions. Side effects, however, convey no mystery and do not open up possibilities of new meanings. One must bear their stubborn absurdity.

Benjamin would ask me to talk, to explain what preoccupied my mind. I tried my best to reassure him, without describing what I was imagining. I tried to remain rational in front of him, but as soon as silence fell, I retreated into a kingdom of distress.

When one is sick, medical terms assume pompous importance and turn one's blood to ice. My being a doctor does not matter to them: Their sternness, which one would like to believe to be fake or farcical, emerges from excerpts of classes and exams, from fragments of limbs and organs exhibited during supervisors' important visits, recalled later as plastic or wax religious offerings: tumid chests, limping hearts or pierced lungs, patched up legs or calcified shoulders, exposed in front of a saintly healer. Then, the words sink in with the renewed seriousness of unequivocal signs, pointing toward misery and the inevitable.

I loved studying medicine; I was a passionate student: the double helix of DNA, the mosaic tiling of cells, the miniature rigging of transmitting networks and pipework filling us with life, the mechanics of lipid canals structuring tiny clocks as tiny as the speck on a speck of dust, the dance of proteins whose deficiency provokes calamities. Later, after the basic sciences, I loved the complex grammar of signs we learned to parse out on sick bodies.

For some years, you see the world through books, and they lead to gurneys and beds. You learn things, forget them, and let yourself get carried away—wandering far from pain, in the realms where nothing dies except to regenerate in accordance with the great biological circle of life. This body of knowledge is intoxicating and makes you admire the beauty of order and logic in illness, until, for the first time, feeling bothered and clumsy, you are confronted by eyes in which one can read the fear of suffering, the anxiety of knowing—anxiety, period.

While sick, I sought the aloofness of the biologist: I sought a place far from myself and descended toward the elementary; I had to remain logical in the confrontation with this tumor that was threatening to tear me to pieces.

Yet, I never consulted medical journals or websites to research the particular type of cancer I had. I preferred to hold on to the vague but precise knowledge the doctors had given me and which had revived my previous education on the subject. I refused to add to the description of frightening symptoms, to read graphs of survival rates or reminders of the carcinogenic effects of the treatments themselves. Didn't I already know enough? In any case, that reality, impersonal and cold as a scalpel, plunged me into a panic if I looked at it too closely. I preferred a whimsical one re-created with certain elements of what they told me. However, at times, I was forced to rein in those flights of fancy: to imagine structures crumbling, rising again, hideously sprawling out; matter ruled by the surge of waves out of my control and that might strangle me in cold blood. I felt as if I were losing my footing: I stood in front of a grave that another person, without a name, goal, or reason, was digging for me, the slab already moss covered. At those moments, courageously avoiding a paralyzing fear, I got a hold of myself. The chemotherapy did its invisible work, as I helped it with all of my will. Surveying the crumbling empire from the headquarters of my mind, I'd consider the army of lymphocytes and white blood cells; I'd orchestrate the battle and give imperious orders to the hierarchy of my immune system like a powerless king. And when fatigue made me more vulnerable, if a feeling of foreboding or despondence emerged, I'd exhort all of these subjects to please remain faithful and defend me. I tried to gain sympathy from them: Please, tiny blood cells, do not desert me!

A patient's universe is an upside-down world. The outside world is pushed away and confined to the far limits of the room. The cosmos resumes a Ptolemaic configuration, and as in ancient times, the sun and celestial spheres start orbiting around the bed, or rather around the pillow.

Not only are its latitudes confounded; daily life also loses all sense of familiarity. Something savage and unpredictable emerges, on the lookout and ready to pounce as soon as you get up and try to leave the room: The mask of slowness cracks; time comes alive again; the energy stirring the people around you is dizzying and jostling.

The treatments I had to undergo not only induce nausea but also take away all taste. The austere shell in which they envelop you creates ideal conditions for a long-term introspective state. You lead a sort of ascetic life and become extremely old before your time. As if a spell were cast on you, you age one lifetime or several: You have a dried-up face like that of a thousand-year-old mummy; you can take only little steps to walk; you need small soft slippers, mittens, and not least of all, a knit cap to cover your head. You are a crippled old man, young at heart, for whom the universe is at low tide, not even missing the ebb of white waters.

When I went to the oncology department for treatments, I had to distance myself from this suspended state. I tried to pretend as if in the present moment, everything was not brutally bizarre and impenetrable: the mechanical attentiveness of ambulance drivers; the silence or chitchat of taxi drivers; mornings in Paris when you no longer needed to go to work but instead toward the fringes of the self, where everything may begin to sway; the hospital lobby packed with people walking around in gowns; the usual hellos from the nurses; the pinkish armchair; and the patients who showed up for treatment that day, some familiar, others never to be seen again.

In the cubicles of the day hospital, each patient sits on a plastic throne, separated from the others by a curtain. An intern asks the usual questions and does not linger. The nurse sets up the IV and bags filled with red, green, yellow, or clear liquids; you watch them empty out without anything, or with barely anything, happening. Once the session is completed, on the return trip, you run into neighbors who don't recognize you, others who stare without saying a word, and others who sympathize with you. Finally, you collapse on your bed. The next few nights will be bad.

After each treatment, it would take several days before I found a peaceful state without unease, and again was able to take refuge between the parentheses.

Being forced to lie in bed for a long time makes you become sensitive to the slightest of movements in and around you. Small adjustments to raise yourself, a sip of water, a stabbing pain, the orchid's flowering on the nightstand—they all have a dense reality. You talk to the space witnessing everything around; to the water that gurgles as it flows from the faucet; to the ceiling, animated with nice monsters—and others not so kind—or with luminous signs dispersing enigmatic messages into the air; to the wall that stoically endures punches you can't throw at anyone else. You encourage a bud, and its blooming makes a morning joyful, a morning, moreover, when everything is going wrong. Low tide has taken away the white waters of the universe, but it has left behind all types of puddles, currents, and rivulets draining whatever is left of you, and you begin to contemplate them with wonder and sorrow.

I kept a few authors close at hand, those who had become my companions during this internal drifting. The shock over, the treatments begun, I began to read a lot, following a thread that was difficult to follow. Above all accounts of unusual and extreme journeys.

I wasn't exploring dangerous lands or confronting unimaginable climate conditions. I was neither persecuted, nor humiliated, nor forced to act against my moral compass to survive; I was only sick. I sought help in those voices that described storms and tremendous suffering, attentive to similarities so as to better understand my own situation and find a way out.

That's how I came to reread the works of Primo Levi, but it was as if I were hearing his voice for the first time.

It's well known that in hell, several circles intersect in a place where you are left alone to fend for yourself, often even against yourself. This illness had thrown me into one of those circles.

During the continuous tightening that strangles you as you fight to survive, your values begin to falter. The grueling months of chemotherapy taught me this. For years, I had done my job healing people. Yet, I no longer had the same compassion for those suffering around me, nor for Benjamin, and this indifference did not make me feel remorse, did not make me feel guilty. I searched in vain for what I had been not long ago, but I found only an empty space, a deflated consciousness.

More than anyone else, Primo Levi made me understand that I was crossing only one meandering aspect of Evil. Beyond the circumstances and peculiarities of abandonment in the concentration camps, he held out his hand to me and warned me to not seek illusory landmarks at the bottom of my destitute state, as they would not bring comfort but only make me suffer more. Rather, Levi encouraged me to put my fate back in the infinite cohort of lives—really to become aware of my humanity.

Of course, the doctors were trying to cure me and not kill me, yet the violence of this disease and these treatments, the inner solitude the doctors did not know how to console, was imposing an experience I knew I might not come back from and that I knew was exceptional.

I'm surprised I noticed so many gestures, glances, silences: I saw the familiar hospital and life itself as I had never seen them before; I saw the half of the world that is invisible to people in good health.

In between two books, read as if I were scrutinizing the flashes of semaphores, sleep would come and take me toward the unpredictable. Sometimes soothing and restorative, it could be disturbed by warped messages or become a festive folly, a carnival diverted toward unknown streets, toward sinister and dangerous alleys, preambles to God knows what.

Dreams were the threshold of the entrance to perilous lands. Waking up, it was difficult to forget their signs and not to take their menacing words as prophetic. I had to remind myself that I was in hell, and that, even if I thought I was going down the right path, everything could be arbitrarily orchestrated for or against me; if a "you are going to die" boomed in a dream, it signified only a bad genie's malice—a false prediction I had to ignore.

Any peace—or rather merely any remission of anxiety—fluctuated and depended upon my giving in to whatever emerged from my dreams and upon how I chose to interpret their words. I was thrown into a journey that in a way resembled the *Book of the Dead*: I staggered on steep cliffs, crossed though marshes, and wandered across steppes, avoiding giant insects and ghost towns. Shadows lurked and crept forward furtively or with grandeur. I had to confront faceless beings and shifting serpents; I needed to listen without believing, to see without being fooled, and above all, to not let myself be overcome by fear.

Nightly dreams took advantage of my helplessness as I lay next to Benjamin. They carried me further away, so much further than the dreams or nightmares of a healthy person.

Benjamin and I crossed this invisible land in parallel, without seeing each other. Sometimes he sensed I had just awoken; he would then caress my arm, hold my wrist, and put his hand on my chest; he would wait for my heart to slow down or for me to tell him about my dream. I'd fall back asleep; he wouldn't. He told me later that afterward he would lean over me in the dark, inhaling the smell of my skin and gently kissing me on the forehead.

He held a constant vigil beside me, yet I barely noticed it.

I'm feverish or I moan with weariness. I don't dare move. I feel the pain preparing its assault; I'm afraid and I call out to the wall to ward it off. Benjamin gets closer to me. Go away. He withdraws his hand. When the torment or nausea forces me to rush to the bathroom, I know he's close to the door, and I whisper not to come in. If my silence lasts for too long, he comes in, squats down, and lifts me up. We go back to bed. His fingers glide over my lips. I cannot speak. My body is calm. That's all that matters.

Embracing each other, we are no longer the home we once were for each other. We no longer have a home.

Benjamin never got impatient, never complained about my mood swings. He would work all day in the library, come back with sweets that I'd grumpily refuse and he would lie next to me as I dozed.

If I felt well enough, I'd talk to him about my reading, some vagaries from my daydreams, describe some patients I'd encountered during chemotherapy, and also those specific gestures, those looks, the indifference, the compassion in others. He would tell me about the research projects he intended to do in Paris, give me news from friends and pass on their hellos, and reassure me that he was coping well. I pretended it was true. I needed to believe that he was serene, that I could count on him.

Later, I learned that certain evenings he would walk around the block two or three times before coming home, he would hang around in supermarkets, and he often missed his stop on the train on purpose. He had been warned: It would be difficult, and he would be alone with the unpleasant role of suffering without complaining. I never saw him cry except the morning of his arrival from the United States, but he would cry with others, when he saw our friends to the door or when my parents visited us; or alone, in the shower. What he was truly experiencing came out only by chance. It was always upsetting to notice how estranged we'd become from each other.

One evening, for instance, I opened the curtain to close the shutters just as he passed by. Upon seeing me, he could not hide a frightened look, the one I'd see on certain faces as I walked on the streets, but his was even sadder and more perturbed than any other. My own reflection on the pane was superimposed on his, and I saw what he was seeing.

Another day, after being half-asleep, I saw him come out of the bathroom naked, his back and buttocks thrown into relief by the light shining on them. My desire for him stirred like a very old, stiff genie who no longer had power, but then it immediately collapsed into lethargy. Having not noticed me, and thinking I was still asleep, Benjamin left the room. At that moment I understood we would lose each other and might never be able to find each other again.

The man in him seemed to have disappeared, replaced by an angel, who had the same features, the same voice, and the same body, but who was no longer the man with whom I had lived for the past ten years. An angel is like a caring person who watches you suffer and die without being able to help you, an immortal being whom you can no longer love, because to love means loving what will eventually die, like you.

It was awful, but it didn't pain me. To stop tormenting both of us, I'd tell myself—without venturing to imagine otherwise—that once the treatments were over, everything would go back to normal.

II

By the following spring, my cancer had been declared in complete remission. The doctors claimed to be optimistic. I'd put on some weight, recovered some strength, and was no longer sleeping all afternoon. My hair was growing back. I felt incredibly energized again.

Anticancer treatments strip you down so meticulously that when you are done, it feels like starting from scratch. You tell yourself it was an initiation and, in this new life, all opportunities will be restored; you will never again miss anything that passes within reach.

Greedy for everything and younger than before without having signed a pact with the devil, I was like a faun emerging from hibernation. Glances from strangers warmed me, as I no longer read in them surprise, embarrassment, or pity. I explored the gulf between the strangers and myself, the calm emanating from the uneasiness of reawakening desires.

Up to that point, I had preferred not to think about what would become of Benjamin and me. I did not want to believe that this shell in which the illness had trapped us, once cracked, would cut us apart. After several weeks, it was obvious: My desire for him was not coming back. I felt only appreciation and the sense, when rejecting him, that I was an ingrate; he had become an absence, and his physical presence, which had once so soothed me, now tormented me with the void it recalled.

Something extremely boisterous stirred in me when he was away. I was assailed by a race of Lilliputians: the tiny arrows of deferred dreams, of repressed or ignored urges, of aimless journeys, all the possibilities you usually ignore or believe are dead.

Lying dormant in me, vagrant and idle desires had not gone away, but rather sought the adventures rekindled in my mind by the illness; they longed for the same focused intensity that had been imposed on me for months—a concentration and a consciousness of being that I had never before experienced. Obviously, I wanted to get better and get over the illness, but something in me struggled to hold on to the vigor, which was slowly waning. It was the unexpected bad side of being healthy.

Others, especially those who have never been sick and can only presume, say that the passion to live comes back after the storm, that I'll want to eat up the sun and the stars. They tell me candidly: It's wonderful; you're in great shape; you're cured.

After a few weeks of health and desires more or less contained in every direction, I had to admit that this rude awakening was not a source of joy. Like a veteran who no longer feels comfortable in his own home, I was missing the time of battles. I was not out of hell yet. I had to embark, without heroism, on a journey back to a place that no longer existed. There had been no metaphysical revolution, no Apocalypse; the sea had not parted. How could I have found this situation poetic? But, I didn't complain. Of course not. Every consultation with the oncologist reminded me how lucky I was. The prognosis for my cancer was not so bad.

To be happy, I would have had to believe that I would lose nothing by getting better. Sickness quickly pushes you along the paths to inner worlds. I wanted to get better but didn't want good health to block the path to the absolute. You find yourself in front of a wall; there is one and only one passageway that nevertheless disperses fears and sculpts a more refined version of the self. I wanted to return without losing any of the simplicity of that refinement. This nostalgia made me a stranger to those who knew me.

Benjamin went back to New York. I wanted to be alone for a while but promised to rejoin him during the summer. The veil of gloom through which we sought each other was not dissipating. We didn't draw any conclusions from this silence between us, and we decided to give each other full freedom to go wherever we pleased.

Considering myself single, I went from one one-night stand to another. Something must have been radiating from within me, an aloof audacity perhaps; or had my descent into hell made me look younger? My success astonished me.

I had an appetite for different bodies, for exotic encounters. My desire no longer had rules or types. I didn't travel on the skin or the bodies of tricks, but rather on the skin of desire itself: I went down the lineage of Noah's sons, and desiring them all, I felt inscribed within me all of humanity—or at least half of it.

Thus, the Coptic Djollali, slender and elusive as a dragonfly, begot Bilal the Algerian; Bilal begot Xavier with the pierced navel, who begot Kolia with areolas as sensitive as water whistles, who begot Florent with the Maori tattoos, who begot the brothers Halim and Kader, who begot Antoine in the early morning on a bridge, who begot Toshio and then Tuan who spoke of the birth of suns, who begot the aptly named Manuel, who begot a native Frenchman whose name I don't remember, who begot the broke Nadir, who begot Léo for a small sum, who begot the supposed virgin Michaël.

Fascinated by the diversity of my desire and how it responded to these unexpected evenings, I felt like a sacred whore.

This lineage of lovers built an invisible bridge—the euphoric encounters, the satiated lust, even the frustration when the object of my desire went his own way—erected a large and solid support in front of me; day and night, these guys embraced me while setting up the ropes that allowed me to move forward over uncertain ground and to reembark on the schooner that would take me far from the sinister Treasure Island where my illness had left me shipwrecked.

Yet, something was missing, and its absence weighed heavily on me: The eruption of libido, the urgency to climax, were the signs of a mourning without a death.

Blade following blade as in a water mill, the wheel brought me water, and I kept repeating: I'm thirsty. I accepted everything that came my way; the water flowed by too quickly; like a pauper to whom one finally says no, I'd lick my wet hands. I didn't know how to quench that thirst.

Nights, roads, and neighborhoods I'd never visited: Glimpsed stairwells and apartments, miserable or posh rooms, unmade beds, mattresses on floors, unfamiliar noises in the early dawn, all formed a realm still too small to accommodate that something, the terrifying echo of that which I had come close to, and which had opened up a space far larger than physical desire.

The old song was heard again. It had often risen in my youth; only Benjamin had calmed this pressing desire to travel. Bugles and drums: Now it was roaring!

I had warned Benjamin that I wouldn't stay long with him in New York. I had an idée fixe: the desert, especially New Mexico's.

My obsession stemmed from old dreams and abandoned travel plans but, above all, from the original enlightenment and the surreal emptiness of time and space I had experienced.

Rarely are we able to silence the world around us; we

would like to, but it chatters within us. Thus we live in a composite world, changing at the whim of our moods and decorated like a Christmas tree with memories from childhood, stories we tell ourselves, and beliefs that we cannot completely drop; a familiar universe we deck out with rags and which, like an old dog, decidedly lacks only the ability to speak.

Suddenly, a loud noise—the big bang—then profound silence. The decorations are blown away. The universe is still there but left bare and imposing like a venerated and taciturn body. Time ceases to exist; until, confronted with this beauty, it shudders in response to whispered voices getting louder, and it slowly swells up with murmurs of wonder.

I was no longer able to make out these murmurings inside me, because the banality of life had begun to chatter again; and this relative deafness was a painful scar, the sign of dulled knowledge, of diminished consciousness.

After reading a book that I will later discuss at length, I started to write an account of my journey within illness; I sought words to open up the immensity I had perceived through the hole closed off by medical terms—a gray mass of pedantic explanations; I tried to define the limits of the hole through language; despite its anguished and dark aura, I wanted to regain the burning sense of *truth*.

I told myself that the desert would bring back the empty plenitude experienced in bed that first morning and, with it, unleash the multiplicity of voices heard during that transitory state, announcing the New. Words did not betray me: the New World, the New Frontier. West! Go west! Go see the colors of creation, the foundation of the earth. When yearning for violence and adventure, when yearning to experience your being, traveling through infinite landscapes makes you believe that you are approaching the origin. There I wanted to track down the New Man.

Even knowing that the myth of the New Man is a poor marionette, a sign on the horizon, beckoning to those left behind, when you have almost nothing else to lose, you are sustained by what is left—words and lies—and by the instinct awoken in the hunter by danger.

In New York, when the taxi dropped me off in front of the building, the super was arranging the trash bins and organizing bundles of newspapers. Next to him, an old Chinese woman was collecting aluminum cans. At the corner of the street, a new building was being constructed, and on the sidewalk across the street, a coffee shop had opened since the previous year.

Benjamin was waiting for me. He had come down to help me bring up the suitcase. We hadn't seen each other in two months. He seemed to have gotten younger by an incalculable number of years.

The studio's decor had hardly changed; it seemed gloomy, small, and tidy, in fact, bare as after the explosion of a neutron bomb. What could have survived of my attachment to this room?

In New York, even more than in Paris, I felt with acute sadness that the shock had displaced something much farther than my body; something had been led astray and was groping for a way to return. The weeks of separation had not healed things between us. Benjamin's presence made me realize how profoundly I had been mutilated. I no longer felt desire for him; nor, for that matter, did he for me.

Holding me in his arms, he sometimes said, "Help me."

I'd say nothing, not reacting.

He'd end up adding, "We have to be patient."

Patient! How could I be patient?

Even if New York fascinates and attracts, while living there you quickly realize that this city, which seems a microcosm of the world, sucks out the desire for the universe and you cannot make love to the cosmos there.

Why should I be patient? Wasn't it time? Time for what? Hadn't I already experienced *everything*? I knew the *truth*. I wanted to share it and didn't know how, or if that was really what I wanted to share. It had been necessary for me to return to Manhattan to understand also that it was a particular truth. Something obvious, which was not easy to talk about, since if I said, I understand that I am mortal, people would answer, Yes, of course; we are too. The truth, however, did not come down to "I'm going to die" or to a peremptory "obviously." The truth was the radical solitude I had experienced when I was condemned; it was a reality with no exit: a simple existential condition. And if, from the moment hope was restored, the violence of my exclusion from humanity through the certitude of death had been attenuated; if, since then, the awareness of that solitude had faded somewhat, both remained in me like a latent pain, a black pebble in a Zen garden—the residue of all consolation.

Benjamin had gone back to his former life, even if more or less without me. When we walked in the parks, in Brooklyn Heights, or along the piers of the Hudson River, when we visited friends or his family, we were walking in the footsteps of what we had been. Funeral bells tolled solemnly everywhere. Benjamin tried to hide his sadness. At times I thought he would have experienced less of a loss if I had died, for I no longer knew how to love him—maybe because I no longer knew how to love at all.

He tried hard to pretend nothing had changed; he knew how to be patient; I couldn't stand that "pretending" or that "patience."

Immobility seemed an unbearable obstacle to the vision of the absolute I had once glanced but that had blurred. I had become a zealot about invoking the hidden face of things. I walked down the streets and kicked the shadows of buildings; I summoned them to life; I aspired to animate matter; whether it terrorize me or strike me down, I didn't care, as long as it radiated the reality that is manifest when you confront your own death. The monumental setting of a city where people, including Benjamin, hypocritically continued calmly to walk, eat, and play thwarted this ecstatic or orgasmic terrestrial supernova.

Ill, I had seen the mental conflagration that destroys and rebuilds everything. On my journey back, I incessantly crossed over this ongoing secret turmoil. How were others not moved by this revolution of being that was in them and around them? Perhaps these people were angels, and my discovery didn't touch them? Perhaps I was the only human being?

Ever since the Victorian era grew neo-Gothic pinnacles, gables, and gargoyles in New York, the city has been sprinkled with angels like the veil of a devout Christian woman of yesteryear. On the facades, at street corners, they keep vigil between the fish scales of skyscrapers. You don't always notice them, but if you are available for a meeting, they promptly stretch out and assault the sky with their swarming or fill it with a deafening silence resonating with calls, sad chants, tears of love.

The invisible flock is at work; they hammer out, restore, sacrifice. You can make them out leaning against pilasters when they are not busy, partly hidden behind a billboard; or you can hear them, disguised as genii of progress and dazzling with promises, defying the shadows of buildings. Suddenly, they go quiet, as soon as the spirit falls from its terrace to be flattened on the mundane. Then you believe you are suffering from intermittent deafness, precisely like the deafness that had loomed over me since the start of my recovery but which still wouldn't go away.

Angels are creatures inhabiting the space between the self before and the self after, creatures bravely chasing away ghosts. Like celestial whales, they roam in the memory of what exploded and swallow what remains of original visions. That's why their song is so violent and so sad.

I was able to detect in this city—more haunting than any place I'd travel to later—the residual waves of my intimate big bang, without really being able to grasp them. They ended up vibrating with desires for new horizons, for endless nights, for universal communions, in the opaque transparency of a destiny that, after all, I preferred to be silent even though kind.

I'd wander the streets until very late; nothing could satisfy me. The former desire for Benjamin had left behind a gap; I was seized by something that expanded and suffocated me, that I could not contain, and made fun of everything.

Travel was the magic word. I did not want to become like the heron in the Sufi story, wishing for bigger fish, all the while catching small ones, not daring to leave the shore.

"Then leave," said Benjamin very fast, and he no longer added, "Help me."

Being sick had made me into an individual with cosmic aspirations. Being healthy may merely have made me egotistical.

The quasi-ecstatic state, this extremely dense void that had frozen me when they told me I had cancer, will have been the most surprising stage of my adventure.

No amorous state, no event, no other journey, had ever produced this exotic feeling caused by the horror of knowing I was condemned: an exoticism that, under threat and on the verge of fragmentation, rejects the confines of any singularity. It seems to me that I had reached the outer limits of a living man's consciousness.

What exactly had I experienced? It's hard for me to put it in words. Fear, willpower, and all desire had been suspended; I had felt a void that completely filled me. I never believed—and I still don't believe—that it was the irruption of transcendence or of a radical altered state. Rather, it was a traumatic vision. I was running into an impenetrable obstacle, radiant, which by eclipsing my ego, had effaced its frontiers without annihilating its presence. In this internal space, I had experienced an un-expected unity in the vision of a self without ego. It was like a kiss from my reassembled consciousness—a kiss of eternity or maybe of adieu; and since I did not die, I must belong to the community of the born-again.

Being born through the spirit seems more than just a passing illumination. The rebirth, about which Jesus con-verses with Nicodemus, and Buddha with his disciples, does not manifest itself as a meteor transforming only the spirit; the complete body participates in the epiphany. Afterward, slowness and silence are needed to complete the progressive transformation of the being.

The slowing down imposed by this second birth is felt for a long time after daily life again imposes its rhythm. It's so difficult getting used to the fast pace of your environment that you think you are suffering from premature aging or from crippling aftereffects; you don't necessarily miss your life as it was before, but rather, you feel a sense of mourning, without really understanding what you have lost.

Maybe because of Manhattan's vibrant movements, I os-cillated between moments when my spirit reopened and I cried in gratitude and hours of panic when the urgency to exist was unbearable. Because of me, we had to spend most of our weekends at friends' homes on the Connecticut coast or elsewhere in New England.

My body needed to expand its physical presence: climbing dunes strewn with prickly marram grass and salicornia, letting myself be hypnotized by the stridulation of cicadas in the elms, catching a glimpse of a seal's snout standing guard, swimming during rising tide until my feet no longer reached the sand, swimming the crawl alone toward the biggest waves.

The presence of others soon bothered me, of those from before especially; and anxiety eroded my pleasures. I had no desire to camp out in this country where I knew people whom I liked but with whom I could not share my precious experience. The pace of their vacation was sluggish, their idleness passive. I didn't want an organized trip to kill time; I wanted to make time last forever.

Benjamin, sensing that I was irritable, would take me out for walks. He was still watching over me even though he was as powerless as others when I slammed doors and left to go get some fresh air.

Most of the time, I found refuge in a museum. In New Haven, Boston, New York, those were the rare places where I was able to take a break from my internal restlessness. I found the slow rhythm I missed inside a calm room, secluded and with little foot traffic, as I became completely absorbed in the contemplation of a work of art.

Insatiable, I continued my journey within old yet fresh emotions, astonished and grateful to be moved, seemingly as never before, by the velvet of a rug painted by Vermeer or a bunch of grapes by Caravaggio, the stricken look of Christ by Memling, a burning ship by Turner, the effrontery of a child by Ribera.

Music also amazed me as if I were discovering it for the first time; the good-byes in *The Song of Earth*, the premonitions in *Winter Journey*, and above all the dawns and mysterious callings in Bruckner's symphonies became unhoped-for refuges where I experienced ephemeral yet immutable epics.

Each visit to a museum, each concert, provoked an aesthetic emotion—an emotion that, without necessarily opening to the mysticism reached through the perception of the cosmos, nonetheless leads to gratitude—an existential clamor; but there was hardly anyone with whom I could speak about this without being exposed to indifference or, worse yet, to polite condescension: Yes, of course, Caravaggio! What a painting! . . . Ah, Mahler!

Must one have spent so many years to be able to understand, to listen, to see? Did I even think before, did I hear, did I see? Was I even alive?

One afternoon, as I wandered around the Metropolitan Museum of Art, I noticed a new acquisition in the Egyptian wing: a fragment, almost the whole portrait of a young princess of the Amarna Period, probably the daughter of Nefertiti and Akhenaten.

This quartzite face is drawn out by a shaven head, overly elongated, as was the custom in royal portraits of the period. The left cheek and temple are eroded; the forehead is damaged; the nose and the chin are broken. The figure no longer has a mouth, but the right ear's concha, perfectly preserved, gives her an attentive air.

During that epoch, a pharaoh had abolished the religion of ancestral gods and founded a new capital in the desert dedicated to the Sun, the sole and unique creator. The pharaoh had reigned for almost twenty years and brought the country to the brink of disaster. Upon his death, the palaces—today found near Tell el-Amarna on the Nile's east bank—were abandoned and the ancient cults reestablished.

This princess had probably witnessed one of the most astonishing revolutions of ancient Egypt. She must have had that fragile sternness of a child grown adult before her time. The spotlight shone on the crystals of quartzite. She seemed to be sweating.

As I stared at her, I came close to tears. Another face had just made hers familiar: the face of a young woman I'd sometimes encountered as I waited for my chemo session.

A little pea had grown in her breast. The doctors had uprooted it, mutilating her; then they had decided to bombard her with cobalt and to water it with poisons to destroy the undetectable rhizomes that might emerge far away, bigger, more virulent. She too was a little princess who had seen her share.

She often talked to her fiancé about her hair. We were both smooth and bald. Would it grow back and how? Would it have the same texture? She said that the color could change. Her teeth worried her even more. She dreaded losing them to radiation; and they do not grow back, not like the tails of lizards or salamanders; and, for that matter, we were not fireproof salamanders; they scorched us with cobalt, but we did not reemerge rejuvenated and transfigured.

The little princess had brought her entourage in the wake of those memories: other patients, drowned since, perhaps.

One man, in particular, whose gauntness had given him the flair of an English aristocrat. Young, he must have looked like Van Dyck's portrait of James Stuart, Duke of Richmond and Lennox, which I had seen earlier that day in the museum and whose ruff, slight tilt of the head, and strabismus, had painfully moved me without my understanding why.

An illness had ornamented this man's neck with cysts. Many treatments had not put an end to these swellings. Several operations had deformed his mandible, which was emphasized by purple scars, and certain movements uncovered hematomas under the scarf or the turtleneck that he was wearing each time I ran into him. A shadow of anxiety hovered around him, the same one that had crept into me when I thought I was done for. A shadow of despair and humility, which place a mask of gray alabaster on one's face.

Six or seven patients would wait together for their treatments. We would look at one another; we had nothing more to say than our pure being, imbued with knowledge and its incommunicability. The day hospital ennobled those who passed through and about whom we did not know much. We had really become living symbols: in transit, condemned but initiated.

Many were lost, anxious, frantic; they must have known they were trapped; they held on stiffly, without enthusiasm, without amiability, or, on the contrary, boastful and masked with a superficial kindness. Some bothered us with their complaining, though we did not let them know. Anguish was heard invading them as soon as they spoke to the doctor. He had only a quarter of an hour to devote to each; in a quarter of an hour, it was necessary to say the Evil in its most precise and sordid form, and to hide the essential: this scandal and this fragility that made strange, absolutely hostile, all that had been thought tamed. The reassurances launched by doctors did not appease the mute panic that could be born listening to others describe the symptoms that we all suffered: toilet bowls soiled with blood, fevers with profuse sweating, bedsores, dried saliva. Faced with the inevitable proliferation of side effects, the doctor imposed brevity.

Others yet would keep their mouths shut, afraid to interfere with the treatment, afraid their indignation would condemn them, that the evil eye would take offense, the eye that spied upon them and would murmur to itself: You're fed up? Just wait for what's up next. . . You're suffering; you're balking? Poor little sweetheart! . . . And you there, don't joke around carelessly. I'll show you!

Others also kept quiet, still not believing that they could be in such a situation.

I said good-bye to the Amarnian princess and hurried out of the museum. The buildings formed ramparts blocking my escape route. Cars and taxis streamed down the avenue. I followed the flow. A little farther, a bastion of lit billboards stopped me. Even without bumping into me, people on the sidewalk annoyed me. I'd have given anything for a stranger's look to say, You are not as alone as you think you are.

Nobody saw me anymore. Since discovering that I was going to die too early, a fact nothing could make me forget, I had been trapped behind a one-way mirror. The confidence and certainties of other people pierced through me. My life vibrated dangerously. I no longer knew how to protect myself. I was being rushed toward death.

Beyond the bastion, a big hotel south of Central Park, stretched out a maze more abstract than that formed by streets, a maze created by passersby, corridors of subway stations, rats crossing the tracks, and subway trains swallowing everything that moved.

Knowledge isolates you inside of a plundered grave, misnames itself lucidity to reassure you. I held this knowledge in horror.

Much later, I went to a private club in the East Village to drink, not far from where Benjamin lived. I had spent a good amount of time there since coming back. At night, you bump into loiterers and lost souls watching porno flicks. Music silences everything else when one is drunk. In this place, sometimes time also stood still.

I stared for a long time at two guys dancing like maniacs. A couple of hours later, I was with one of them on 158th Street, north of Harlem.

I woke up in the early morning, alone in a bed. Light diffused from an interior courtyard; an air-conditioning unit hummed in another room. I went to take a piss; a blurred grayness moved around me; I had drunk too much. I went back to bed without looking for the guy. I was stiff. It's true we hadn't fucked gently.

Noses, ears, throats, and all these lips every which way. Hanging on to each other's necks, legs in the air—if only we could have stayed like that, suspended by invisible vines or by levitation. We'd ended up falling back on the bed. I'd pressed his face against the mattress to kiss him; he'd pushed me back to catch his breath and attack me. At one point, astonished and delighted, he'd said: You looked so tame! And then he'd relaunched his hands at me in an enthusiastic approach. Squeezing my hips or my shoulders, roughing them up, he seemed to be an expert on navigating open seas.

His dick was a separate being. I introduce you to my twin brother, he said mischievously in the elevator where we had started making out. Nice to meet you. It stood upright with elegance, like a classy mutineer. In front of me, under me, above me, this stubborn brother unknotted the rigging and unfurled the sails of night, swallowing me, fascinating me, even scaring me a bit, like Jim Hawkins in his apple barrel. Whirling around a ferocious need, the twin brother had unleashed a powerful swell. To live. There was lightning and thunder.

The guy must have been asleep on the living room's sofa; I heard feeble cracklings coming from the TV set.

He wanted to be an actor, he had told me. At first, he would star in porno flicks to pay the rent to the guy putting him up.

Later, noises coming from the kitchen woke me. He told me his future plans after a while of sipping coffee mixed in with kissing.

Nothing was free here; everything had a price. And then, the language and mentality were different. Yet, you could certainly make your mark. He had come from Haiti a year before; he was so very pleased to speak with someone who understood him. Those people, he said referring to Americans, were not like the Haitians or the French; they did not know how to enjoy life. Sure, he was going to show these fuckers how they fuck in Haiti. They had predicted he would become a star.

That morning, he had a meeting with a producer in a hotel near Columbus Circle. It was already late. We could meet toward noon, eat something, go for a walk in Central Park, just as he had suggested the night before, and then come back to make out in the apartment. He had always dreamed of having a French friend and spending a summer in Paris. Of course he would come visit, as soon as he had the means.

Ironically, or on a romantic impulse, or by chance—

I'm not sure—he set a date on the Bethesda Terrace, in front of the fountain depicting the healing Angel. He might be late, but he would come. He was a man of his word, a practicing Baptist, from a liberal congregation, of course, and above all, a servant of God.

I went down Saint Nicholas Avenue from 158th Street all the way to Central Park, strolling through neighborhoods that I didn't know.

Sitting in the sun in front of the fountain of the Angel, I waited. Three hours later, I was still waiting. I knew that one-night stands usually don't lead to anything other than a good time and disappointment, but it was not for him that I was waiting by then.

The very long parenthesis opened the night before had closed itself. During a couple of hours, I had forgotten the little princess, the gaunt gentleman. The last time I had seen both of them, their cancers had not been in complete remission. Despite having finished treatments, they would need a tougher protocol. They had each intimated they had a chance of getting cured, but a very slight one.

The Angel offered up the lily of her aloofness. The sculptor Emma Stebbins had dedicated this work to her sick companion, a woman. *De profundis*. Beautiful Angel, if you could only do something for us. On that day, it was covered with the usual rows of pigeons and surrounded by tourists. It didn't chase away my ghosts. The guy was not going to show up.

The servant of God probably had better things to do with his producer. Had he perhaps lied or forgotten? Was this maybe the very message of the emissary? A chance meeting opens up time as Jehovah did the sea; you move forward between parted waters, admiring the fragility of intimacy; then once all have reached the shore, the tide swallows up the hope that magic could have everlasting effects. The only memories I had left were of the morning's passion and of tenderness.

I bid farewell to the Angel and left. I gave a bill to a beggar smiling in the sun. To give thanks to the guy who had become a ferryman without knowing it.

I wished these alms would also absolve me. I was suddenly ashamed. I had not even warned Benjamin about my little adventure.

I walked to Chelsea Piers, where Benjamin and I met sometimes.

Like all jetties on earth, those enclosing Manhattan with a rim of concrete and wood are conducive to daydreams. It's obviously no longer the time when the young Redburn looked for a job as a sailor on his first crossing, when old Melville worked as customs inspector. The forest of masts, the impatience to seize passersby with dreams of the high seas, no longer exist. Rather, the docks seem forsaken. Aside from some yachts and abandoned warehouses, great flights have to find their momentum starting from pylons and pontoons adorned with tires, where seabirds fly above, watching over departures as in the past.

In the confusion of gulls, terns, and shorebirds; in the muddle of ascents and descents, of fights with beaks and jousting wings, of invisible coils, of bird droppings, and of crushed shells; in this weaving against a background of buildings, one finds the logical traces of nature ready to take over the planet from humans once more.

Certain species—petrels and cormorants—lead your thoughts upstream. I walk upriver, through Riverside Park in the north, and leave behind the Cloisters. Underneath the Henry Hudson Bridge connecting Manhattan to the Bronx, a vista opens up; in this city, it is the most powerful launchpad for the imagination in my opinion.

A body of rock rises from the bank lapped by the Hudson, giving a glimpse of the deep foundations of the borough. You realize that Manhattan rests on a half-buried giant, whose chest emerges here like the stern of an Olympian ship.

The city seems incidental on this titanic body: It's but a menagerie of actresses at a premier, shimmying around on stage and dabbling at their roles, without succeeding in impressing the director of the play. I had indeed become a demanding and blasé director, and I was impatient: I wanted to see the presence that had existed before mankind swelled up; I wanted to feel the flux of this inhibited cosmic force.

Visions are caught by their corners. One just needs to pull gently to unravel them from the spool of dreams, as one untangles poetry from the skein of words. In this way, a fragment from a boulder or the droppings from seabirds become accomplices of the whole universe.

The last few times we went to the river in Chelsea, Benjamin would sit watching the sunset. I'd go for a walk. We were no longer united by the beauty of the scenery nor, for that matter, by anything else. His silence held me back from giving my visions their true amplitude. Their songs called to me. Benjamin was a mooring rope I yearned to break off.

The yearning to travel stemmed not from a simple desire to leave but from a need for a radical exoticism. It was as if I were in a hurry to die. I had never experienced anything as intense as what the illness had made me feel. Maybe I was just suffering from the affliction of certain mystics, and I was dying from not dying.

When I got home later, Benjamin did not ask me any questions; he simply said:

"It's best that you leave."

I took off for New Mexico the next day.

Near Albuquerque, the Sandia Mountains overlook the Rio Grande Valley. They outline the savage body of a wildcat whose limbs rest on the edges of landing strips, whose coat of ochre-pink rocks is spotted by groves of juniper bushes.

Immediately, the mountains took a liking to me. The thousand eyes of the beast gave me a welcoming wink.

It was the distant cousin of its New York accomplices, birds and the rock titan, all members of the same mysteriously powerful and discreet gang by virtue of the code of silence that rules this vast mafia beyond the control of mankind. The big cat on alert watched me prowl around and look for the *eternal*, leading me through its terrain—I'd soon understand its game—to remind me that the Great Earth, this unflappable Stoner communicating with us through heightened states of our souls, does sometimes level all suffering.

Albuquerque stands in the middle of a convergence of highways spreading its roads out over the southwestern United States, toward the gypsum dunes of the White Sands desert, toward the warm horizons of Chihuahua, and toward the legendary South. New Mexico's state nickname sends out an ambiguous warning: land of enchantment, the land of tabulae rasae, of destitute pueblos and mythic cities of gold, of mystic hippies and nuclear testing.

At the heart of this convergence, I briefly had the oceanic impression that I was really a New Man, coming back from the dead like the resurrected in Ezekiel's vision. I was happy, so happy to be on the verge of fulfilling so many tacit promises.

During the flight, longer because a violent storm had delayed my connection in Atlanta, I had retraced—with the help of guides and books—migration patterns going backward to the North. History is a meditative practice, isn't it? With it, you can create mandalas of dreams and crack open a present that is too obtuse. Following the Native Americans' exodus, you go from detours to dead ends, from wars to epidemics, toward the migration that traversed the Bering Strait, supposedly. Group of peoples coming from Asia took the necessary leap of adventure to embark on a one-way journey so fascinating that we shroud it in myths.

There are places—in other words, moments—favorable to setting the sails of history. Spaces allowing such moments are sacred.

I hadn't considered staying in Albuquerque. I had been told that it was just a pit stop on a journey either north toward the Rockies or west toward the desert. My plan was to drive the roads of New Mexico and the contiguous states in a spiral trek. To an observer looking from the sky, my journey would have formed a mysterious shape on maps, like those of Nazca. I loved this idea.

In the end, I did not trek along a spiral path to visit the region but rather trekked out from Albuquerque, to which I remained attached as the ball in a cup-and-ball toy. Not because I liked this city but rather because I came back to see a guy I met the first night I got there.

I was a balloon of dreams; a stranger sufficed to weigh me down.

Victor talked a lot and asked a lot of questions. After trying to sell me a Peruvian knit hat in the mall where he managed a stand for the summer, he let me know that he preferred older men. Daddies, to be exact. My age? That of his father. That stung; later I almost forgot about it.

He dragged me to the apartment he shared with two roommates, who were absent that night. The other times, when I came back to Albuquerque to see him, we met at my hotel. He wanted to be discreet. He wasn't out of the closet.

His smile revealed a charming gap between the upper front teeth; he was well built and had dark brown curly hair, and his stance reminded me of a young bull.

The first time, he asked me to look away while he undressed, and he covered himself as he got into bed. I pulled the sheets back, suffocated by the ruggedness emanating from him. The air blowing from a fan flapped a strand of his hair. He closed his eyes. For a long time, I caressed the small love handles that rounded his hips, caressed from his calves to his buttocks, from his shoulders to his stomach. I dug in with both hands to feel the depth of his young body's confident calmness, to feel the sweetness of his naïveté; through my palms I buried myself in him. He didn't whine, didn't complain, but shivers

73

ran up and down his muscled limbs.

I was a water diviner who believed I had lost my powers, but stretched out my fingers once again to call forth the flow of subterranean waters, to recognize the convolutions of hidden networks, to taste the freshness of life and predict the mouths where it will well up.

Waking up the next morning, I remembered I was in one of the world's navels.

The room was a mess, our clothing spread out on the floor. The night before, we had had some pizza—its box was resting on a chair—and we had drunk a bottle of wine, empty now next to a cactus in its planter on the windowsill. The open arms of Rio de Janeiro's Christ the Redeemer, figured in the poster in front of the bed, welcomed us.

We continued to make out and hang around in bed all morning. He didn't needed to be at his stand until afternoon. I listened to the inventory of his wanderings and adventures. He had a real knack for storytelling and the boastful confidence of coy people. In a town like El Paso, where he had grown up and where it was better to be careful about one's sexuality, he had been able to pride himself in his exceptional experience for an American his age and in having seen up close the depravity that certain family men hide. That's what he said.

As for me? I didn't feel like sharing all the details

of my sexual history. He wanted to know if I had a boy-friend. I replied with a shake of my head.

"I see, not too faithful. Like the French in general," he said, with a knowing and disapproving look on his face.

I was not in the mood for a preachy speech, even if it would mean adding some spice to our lovemaking. Maybe my sense of humor was absent. A little annoyed, I explained to him my situation, and the origin of the scars that had intrigued him the night before.

"I feel sorry for your boyfriend," he concluded.

Yet, he wanted to know about the details of my illness and started talking about his mother, who had suffered from breast cancer two years before and had survived it. He thought my story was amazing: a sick doctor, what a great subject for a book!

Victor reacted in the same way as many of my lovers: His curiosity, at once unconcerned and interested, showed the extent to which he did not see the fear I didn't speak of. This ignorance, which hurt me or angered me in other people, made him more seductive, painfully seductive. Like a nimble young bull, he was getting ready to attack the small forts of the land. He had the type of courage fed by repressed fears and by poorly healed wounds.

Victor listened to me with the look of a tightrope

walker or a warrior, but while defying the universe, he talked constantly about his parents. Thanks to a scholarship, he had started studying at the University of New Mexico but intended to transfer to Harvard or preferably to Yale. Son of immigrant parents and descendant of Native Americans, he was going to become a playwright. In this country, being half–Native American, half-Mexican, does not really give you a chance to partake in the American dream; you have little chance of success unless you have the wings of an eagle, are stubborn as a bull—unless you are a sort of sacred chimera fluttering about boldly. He had no doubts about his energy or his lucky stars.

He listened to me from above, jousting with the future, where death did not exist. He joked around and underplayed my most intimate thoughts. Like a child marveling at clay fledglings but killing birds in a tree with a slingshot, he was amazed by the nonsense and exploits of my work in the ER, which I openly shared with him.

The other nights, I noticed that what he liked most of all was to watch me, that he was more interested by the way I got pleasure from him than in having an orgasm himself. Young people take that type of pleasure for granted, and it drove me mad. The gap between our ages and expectations reminded me of that "thing" I was seeking but that had been absent since the beginning of my quest. At first, I thought I had found the fountain of youth, but it was the feeling of being old, very old, that dominated me each time I saw him.

By considering the universe in the abstract, you become a somewhat hollow giant. Victor had clear ideas. Seeing his determination and his ambitions, I felt sickly, stiffened by the blood of daydreams. I was the man of bronze wounded in the ankle by Jason; I was losing my life-force and could not hold on to it.

I confronted Victor rather than hugging him; I spent myself as if, to celebrate life through his body, I had to be prodigal with mine, as if, to find the strength to believe in the future again, I had to dissipate myself through a desperate potlatch. He would remain quiet, which was rare for him, in the face of my passion.

Only once he said:

"What energy you have!"

Energy? I was draining it, I was exposing myself to danger. Yes, I was rushing toward death. And as if he had read my thoughts, he added with a smile:

"All the same, be careful. Don't die in my arms."

I traveled across the region by car without lingering in the towns, which were all disappointing.

In the Valley of Tears

Santa Fe is no longer the mythic crossroads of New Spain and the pilgrimages of the famous archbishop from Auvergne, founder of the diocese. Santa Fe is only a Saint-Tropez of the desert. Taos, a summer and a ski resort, is even more disappointing. Farther up, on the plateau surrounded by the Sangre de Cristo Range, you are halted by the narrow gorge of the Rio Grande. At this point, the river, which cuts through the volcanic plateau and flows three hundred meters farther down, opens up onto a more distant land; moving freely past dams as it flows toward the south, it traverses the desert without refreshing it, to become the watertight border between Texas and Mexico. It changes its name like souls of the dead crossing over to the beyond as it flows into the estuary at heroic Matamoros and the Gulf of Mexico.

Surviving here and there throughout the region are those clichéd images hawked by westerners and guides and glimpsed in mirages. You tend to forget them as you travel north toward counties with sacred assonances—Rio Arriba, San Juan, Montezuma, paths of names leading toward another country within itself. The road is roughened up by dark elbows of pine forests and horns of whitewashed cows' skulls, by reservoirs of pure colors, drowning it in cinnabar and orpiment; or, hesitant and dusty, it tightens its bend around bizarre rock formations, follows ancient sanctuaries and hostile overhangs.

I didn't understand why I felt such a calm and sad pleasure wandering the routes lined with the names of vanishing tribes, dying towns, and slumbering religions. I didn't understand that I was being welcomed by the only wealth that remained: spaces emptied out, just like the dreams in my hospital bed, where words in ashes waited to be spoken.

In between visits to Albuquerque to meet Victor, I'd spend solitary hours at the edge of rocky valleys punctuated by juniper trees, next to dried up streams; or sitting behind cheap motels to gaze at the parade of prairie dogs or at cautious wild rabbits hopping from one bush to the next and, even, to follow with my eyes the zigzags of small beige-and-turquoise-striped lizards, like those I used to chase as a child.

As soon as I was alone, I was seized by a need for simplicity and passionate embraces that couldn't be satisfied anywhere. I loved humanity and the universe in all its variety and would have liked to know all the epochs of Man's history, all the cultures and all the languages. I would have wished to disappear as a result of knowledge, like Wells's traveler with his time machine.

No matter where I went, I sought nature's complicit nod, like the one I had gotten from the big wildcat of the Sandia Mountains on the day I arrived. The gang was suspicious: Except for some lizards, I didn't spot any signs of the conspiracy.

For the wildcat's thousand eyes to penetrate me and make me see and love without hoping to lose myself, I needed to squelch my anxiety.

For the time being, I was in the midst of living the pains of a second birth, constantly looking behind me, fascinated by the light that gave birth to me and by the place in it from which I believed truth and radiance emanated.

It was the temptation of the desert: I missed the feeling of utter destitution in the lowest state of fatigue when you are involved, against your will, in the adventure, when you are stripped naked by it and you must abandon yourself or perish. Sometimes, it occurred to me that I needed to relive the extremity of my exhaustion without worrying about coming back. I missed the unattainable place of unimaginable orgasmic bliss where birth and death touch each other.

Once, I had tried to explain that to Victor. He thought that, despite what I had gone through, I maintained a very romantic view of death.

"If you go too far, you die, and that's it. Every year, there are fools who die in the desert without wanting to. And in the desert or elsewhere, no one wants to die, right?"

One day, shortly before my departure, on a road leading to Arizona, I stopped at a Navajo reservation where Victor had told me one could see petroglyphs—prehistoric drawings found throughout the region—not featured in guidebooks and which represented rather unusual geometric compositions.

I left the car at the bottom of a small hill and went up toward a rocky plateau, avoiding sagebrush because I had been warned snakes rested in it and taking some detours to see up close the rare yellow and mauve flowers that hadn't been scorched. On the horizon, only mountains, crows, and vultures swirled around. On the ground, some coarsely carved flint stone and some small closed geodes. It was toward the end of the day; it was very hot.

Shattering the silence, a motorcycle passed nearby. Suddenly, I felt completely alien in this landscape, a banal awestruck tourist facing an impervious beautiful scene, where human consciousness is akin to a shooting star crossing the sky in plain daylight. I was a city dweller dressed as a city dweller; I stood in the desert like a feather fallen from the sky, and just like a feather, I had almost gotten stuck on the melting asphalt of the pavement.

To become one with the universe, you have to wander, crawl, thirst; your eyes have to burn; your sweat has to scorch your face; you have to seek the shade, to apprehend solitude, and to regret with all of your might the fact of being there; you have to understand the horror of the desert and to know its hold on you; and then, you need luck to survive the experience.

I wasn't truly touched by the majesty of the vast landscape, as I would be, three or four years later, when I came back to the region with Benjamin.

I remember that on the plateau, while taking pictures of the petroglyphs I had found after meandering around the rocks, I was overtaken by a fear I had never experienced before.

To seek that which had manifested itself only once could only be sacrilegious—a masquerade. I shouldn't desire anything. Neither to survive, nor to die, nor to understand.

The journey begins when you can no longer choose. My desert was my hospital bed.

III

The oncologist had scheduled a follow-up in September. Six months had passed since the end of treatments, and I intended to go back to work in the ER.

I returned to Paris without seeing Benjamin. The many roads of New Mexico had not given me a new direction to follow. Victor had not brought me to a calm port. The future was only a bride's wilted bouquet.

Soon after my return, I finished writing the story I'd been working on intermittently during the summer—writing as do so many travelers who are nostalgic for their experience of hell. But as I have said before, I had started writing mainly as a response to a book I had read some months before.

In 1977, in Germany, a book was published by a young unknown author, Fritz Zorn, who had just died from cancer. It was an autobiographical essay, *Mars*, which took up the old debate about the psychological causes of cancer.

Raised on Zurich's Gold Coast in a comfortable milieu, Fritz Zorn leads the bland and solitary life of a passionless teacher until the age of thirty. In the mid-seventies, he finds out that he is suffering from a malignant lymph node. He begins medical treatment and psychoanalysis simultaneously.

During chemotherapy sessions, you often hear: What do you expect? This cancer is caused by all the suffering you have endured and kept inside. When a serious illness concludes a life ravaged by frustrations, trials, and mourning, it becomes the most instinctive explanation.

Once you discover that you have cancer, you need to try to put out the fires set by the whys without explanations. If the causes are clear—cigarettes, alcohol, all kinds of excesses, or genetics—one can drown in guilt, regrets, or rant about fate; but if you cannot blame excess nor genetics, nor any other cause, if you hear that there are not known causes, and if even your age cannot give a vague explanation, then you expose yourself to the hammering of whys.

Zorn's logic, inscribed within the thinking of partisans of the theory that cancer has psychosomatic origins, is simple: My cancer, he writes, was formed from swallowed tears, from suppressing too many conflicts, and from hostility against my parents, against my environment, from having suffered disabling sexual repression and from allowing all desire and life itself to get snuffed out.

He also dreams that the only path to a cure is through the dissection of his education, the analysis of his milieu, turning this internalized violence against them to escape their internalized murderous hold. My cancer, he writes further, is only the consequence of this dead state in which my education trapped me, and if I die from the cancer, one could say that I was educated to death: I must throw in the fire this bourgeois upbringing if I want to heal.

A comforting attitude because of the solution it offers, if it were not under the threat of an unavoidable death sentence. In the case of Zorn, the illness progresses relentlessly, and the clarity he brings to his condition ends up adding to his suffering. According to him, understanding the cause of the Evil he is suffering from does not take away from the fact that every cell in him has been poisoned by tears.

Written during the last year of his life, *Mars* bears the mark of an insurmountable scandal, of a terrifying anger.

Zorn declares a state of total war, and just as he had been careful not to waver from the upbringing that stifled him, he meticulously carries the blaze to every corner of his already burning house. He is keen to destroy himself, and having been a quiet boy too long, he sets fire to peace along with his life.

Like Balthazar Claës, the alchemist in Balzac's novel, the restrained, reserved, and measured Zorn becomes a fire thief, a metaphysical terrorist. He consumes himself in his quest to find the morbid origins of cancer, its cure through unconscious powers, just as Balzac's hero in his quest for the absolute ruins himself and dies, convinced he is on the brink of discovering the secret of the universe. A quest for an explanation and a cure, brimming with suffering and despair.

I was shaken by this book. And who wouldn't be, in the face of the tragedy of a man who, at the moment of his death, discovers that he hasn't lived? Every patient, especially when young, lives this nightmare in varying degrees.

Identifying with him was unavoidable. Even if we did not come from similar social backgrounds, Zorn was almost my age and was diagnosed with a lymphoma just like me.

In my case, the doctors had been more or less optimistic. In thirty years, there had been great progress
in treatments. You can be cured, they had assured me.
Uncertainty remained, however, and so did the whole
mystery of why. Around me, some people proposed advice and volunteered exhortations: It was tedious to hear
"fight" because, while sick, you feel that conscious willing
is impotent in activating a life-force that does not necessarily save you. Others offered wild interpretations. According to them, not only would I have to go through the
chemo treatments; I also needed to ask myself: Why did I
get this goddamned cancer? A question that brought up
a swarm of agonizing memories and resentments that I'd
believed had been healed.

My relationship with my family had not been simple. To be able to live out my sexuality peacefully, even
normally, in a loving relationship, had been a long battle.
I didn't need tactless people to remind me that I had re-
tained my share of tears, sometimes unconsciously, which
perhaps were eating me up. Yes, maybe my body was de-
stroying my life because, at bottom, something, someone,
a force, could externalize itself only by killing me. Maybe
this illness was an escapee from my unconscious against
whom I was powerless.

If I let my thoughts go down that slippery slope, I
would immediately land in a circle of hell more dreadful

than the one I was already in. Whenever I started sliding down toward that circle, I would pull myself back with all my might and try to remain in a state of unknowingness, or let's say in an obstinately self-deprived mental state, in an unwillingness to understand. To be at peace, I needed to find refuge in an inner poverty, where one can admit only impotence and vulnerability without complacency. An attitude of passive resistance more than resignation.

I followed Primo Levi's example. Later, when I was in remission, when I was able to write, I tried to analyze more coolly what I had gone through, but during the journey itself, I repeated to myself the warning a cynic threw at Levi's face when he entered the concentration camp: "*Hier ist kein Warum.*" Here there are no whys.

This sentence, uttered in a universe governed by a malevolence, which I had obviously never experienced, summed up one of the possible attitudes for survival in the face of Evil, and I made it mine.

Contemplating the absence of meaning allowed me to survive spiritually what I felt lurking inside of me. Analysis or anger, like that of Zorn, paralyzed and led me toward drowning.

A work by Turner depicts what was at stake during my battle with the illness. I had seen it again that summer in

New Haven's Yale Center of British Art on a day I had ditched some friends.

This painting, which prefigures Turner's late seascapes, is known under the title *Wreckers—Coast of Northumberland, with a Steamboat Assisting a Ship off Shore.* Confronting a raging sea, the wreckers wait for the beaching of a boat drifting offshore without sails. Bandits organized in gangs to pillage shipwrecked vessels and victims, the wreckers wouldn't have hesitated to light lanterns on dangerous shores or to launch flares in stormy weather to lure ships toward reefs.

In Turner's painting, a steamboat weathering the storm helps the sailboat in distress. The painter leaves the scene unresolved. The sea and the storm will eventually decide the outcome.

The two authors I've just mentioned played an almost Manichaean role during my long haul as a patient. Primo Levi, the moralist steamboat, guided and helped me return to my humanity; he conquered internal storms and saved me from spiritual shipwreck. Fritz Zorn's despair isolated me and cast me off to my fate; he threw me into a well of insurmountable solipsism, smashing against the absurdity of Evil. Zorn's book prevented me from finding any solace, in spite of everything, in what I had experienced; he eclipsed drunken confrontation with the unknowable.

I couldn't in any way tame the savagery of this fate, of its jolts that no one knew how to predict; but the vagueness in my gut had led to a lucid psychic space where consciousness manifested itself without fear in the knowledge of its own impotence.

That space had saved me more than once from sheer panic. I wanted to honor it in writing.

Shortly after I'd finished writing my story, there was a dramatic turn of events.

A follow-up scan had revealed an anomaly; my doctors immediately ordered a type of gamma scan more precise than the original test. The radiologist confirmed the presence of a suspect area. The result was ambiguous, but one could strongly fear a recurrence, he said, while pointing out a cluster of converging spots that looked like a black hole on the image. To be certain, we had to wait a couple of weeks and do another scan to follow the evolution of the lesion.

The image he had shown me depicted a homunculus sprinkled with dark spots and resembling a sewing pattern studded with pinholes. I was this pierced figurine, and an unwitting pioneer, I had been sent out again in a space probe to the outer edges of the known universe.

The illness had become deadly again. The purpose I

had tried to find in this cancer seemed to me like a pitiful lie and the interior journey, the quest and the story that I had used to transform it, like blinding enchantment.

Inside of me, the gaping chasm opened up again, but neither rebirth, nor light, nor salvation emerged from it, only implacable fright: the uttermost certainty that I was done for.

I had just entered into a circle like none I had entered before. The most difficult leg of the journey was about to begin.

When I left the hospital, I was on a sloping sidewalk. I was a pile of sand blown by the wind, a crumbling silhouette that my spirit could no longer shape into a stable form.

That night, after having spent a lot of time hanging out in bars, I found myself in a stranger's home. I had been so afraid to end up alone that night.

In front of his house, he had forewarned me:

"Don't be afraid of my tenant."

He pushed his door open, the parquet floor creaked, and a skeleton in the entryway pointed its outstretched arm toward me. A device of props and pulleys controlled this contraption.

"The breath of death is on you," the guy claimed, pulling me toward him to kiss me.

His mother was from Normandy, he told me somewhere along the line, and on that side, generation after generation, they had been wizards. Even today, in his family's village, people were afraid of his very old grandfather. According to what a fortune-teller had claimed, he also had powers, but they manifested themselves differently than in casting spells: He had become a sculptor.

While undressing, he slowly swiped his finger over the scar on my belly but didn't ask any questions. Later, at a crucial moment, he dug his fingers into the scar as if wanting to disembowel me, going into ecstasy:

"I love it, love it; it turns me on."

Rather than energizing me, he had usurped my forces.

Leaving his house the next morning, I was overcome with panic. I felt trapped. It was beautiful outside, but tears rained inside of me.

I let Benjamin know the results of the medical checkup; he suggested he come back to Paris. For what? Benjamin could no longer help me.

Fritz Zorn's words came back to me. Was he right? Wouldn't the illness liberate me in the end? Throughout the summer, hadn't I called upon my own death? I pulled myself together. I had been foolish enough to believe that I could turn an absurdity that kills you into an illusory initiation. You wanted to shape me, the evil eye said, and seduce me by putting on prudish airs. You thought you had gotten rid of me? I was always on your tail, and you knew it.

So as to no longer hear its voice, I took some sedatives and buried myself in bed.

In the Valley of Tears

After the shock from the news, I looked for help among my friends. I tried to decipher the truth in their eyes. Some condemned me; others saved me. Blind to myself, I wanted to believe that healthy people, especially close friends, were visionaries. I'd almost ask them to read my tarot cards. Of course, none of them would have told me: You're screwed! But I surmised as much from the looks of some. You must be at peace with yourself to be sure that others don't know more than you do, and to understand that they are going through the same night as you are.

I couldn't bear to be alone, and I couldn't stand the company of others, even of strangers. As soon as someone asked me what I did for a living, I would remember in a flash that I no longer did anything, that I wasn't healing anyone, that I had lost Benjamin, and that I was going to die because I was a vulnerable doll, at the mercy of any quack wizard.

Anxiety ran amok in the streets; you could see it and hear it everywhere: on unmasked faces, on the swirls of trash and leaves, through the openings of plastic bags.

This time, I experienced the fear of a cancer spiraling out of control. Nothingness verging forever toward terror.

Zorn and I, and all those condemned to face this situation, suffer from the same Evil: It's impossible to sustain a vision, even obliquely, of that which radically burns. When confronted with the unbearable, emotion and reason make the mind oscillate between an attempt at an honest vision and its mitigation by a thought, a poetic device, a rhetorical move. Metaphorical, lucid, logical screens: Facing this horror, the cocoon from where you believe a pure vision can be sustained inevitably becomes opaque like the lovers in *The Garden of Earthly Delights*.

My doctor had reminded me that treatment was plausible in the case of recurrence, certainly arduous and inconsistently effective, but given my age, it could be given a try. I have no idea how I would have reacted had he told me that there was no possible remedy.

So, I had to start again.

To prepare myself, I reached out to my friend Primo Levi, but his voice no longer consoled me. I perceived only the despair of what he'd seen and of all that he hadn't seen, his implacable lucidity about the human condition.

I was immersed in a circle of hell unfolding upon a desert of doubt without poetry. No more daydreams, no more friends, no more books. I was a perpetually descending yo-yo with no way to stop the inexorable unraveling of my thoughts, except for sleep bogged down in anxiolytics and sedatives. I would have given anything to be magically saved, especially at night after waking up from a nightmare.

Dramatic turns of events are sometimes followed by a *deus ex machina*. In my personal drama, it took the form of a lanky chap, wearing combat boots and a tight jean jacket.

Upon writing this, it seems like a plot twist in an airport novel. And, in fact, our unplanned meeting happened at a train station.

Fall was in the air; it was even a bit cold on the platform of the commuter station where I got off at the same time as he did. We had checked each other out for a long time in the train car. His face carried traces of something rarely seen out in the open—the harsh tenderness of guys who may have little but are full of dreams. I decided to approach him once I saw his smile when he heard a little girl make a witty remark to her mother. His name was Sami, and unfortunately, he had to go to work.

We met each other that night at a café near the Gare du Nord. His hand shook so much that he had to hold on tightly to his spoon by driving it down into his cup and stirring; even his wrist trembled so uncontrollably that he had to grab it to keep it still. The cold was not the culprit for this strange behavior.

He lived with his sister, his only family; loved sled dogs; and had a passion for soccer. He worked as a salesman at a sports store, but a coach had just scoped him out during a semiprofessional game; he was supposed to play soon for the team's manager, with a possibility of an offer.

Rather quickly, he felt at ease with me and told me stories from his teenage years, social services, and foster families. After having laid out his "pedigree"—the word he used—he added: "It's your turn."

Dishing out some details about my life, I started to talk about the momentous event that had turned it upside down. I had done this often during the past summer. Each time with some boasting, I believe. Now, there was no longer any victory or heroism in the telling.

"Are you cured now?" he asked.

"Not exactly."

He became very attentive. I had to elaborate.

Later, he laid down his big white body on the bed. Long, strong, elegant legs extended out from his Mickey Mouse boxers. He held me in his arms while kissing my hair. I was a little man, just a little man, who was going to die. He held me tighter and covered me with his whole body. He climbed frenetically up a strange mountain to make a bizarre pilgrimage—to become enamored of someone whom, by fate, one must leave behind. I heard his heartbeat clearly, forcefully. I don't know how long we stayed that way. Until the unexplainable happened.

He was going up this internal mountain; suddenly, he stopped, sat up, and became a prophet.

"No! You will get cured," he said moving back a bit, "and you will travel even more than before. You will get cured! And soon, you will start helping people again, lots of people. . . . I'm not the one saying this to you. It's not me! I don't know why, but you have to believe me."

I feel him looking intently at me, worried that I'm going to make fun of him.

"I believe you, Sami."

He says again with a trembling voice:

"It's not me saying this. . . . You are cured!"

He lays down on his back again. Whatever possessed him suddenly had drained him out. I don't dare to touch him.

As skeptical as I was at the time, his words disturbed me. His voice had changed in that instant. He had seemed possessed by a conviction stronger than the simple wish for my cure, going beyond compassion.

"You know," he said a couple of minutes later, "that's not the first time that's happened to me. When my best friend lost his mother last year, I saw her floating above him. She wanted us to understand that we shouldn't be sad. . . . You don't believe me, right?"

He wanted me to believe him unconditionally. I thanked him, a bit embarrassed.

"No, don't thank me. I have nothing to do with it. I really want you to feel safe."

"I believe you, Sami. Really," I told him.

I got closer to him. Soon after, we cuddled up and he fell asleep. I watched him in the dim light. I was relieved; I didn't know what would happen to me, but I was no longer afraid.

Prophets only exist through the echo in those they meet. This little prophet told me not only that I had nothing to fear, but also that *all* I had lived through was real.

Maybe I had just taken comfort in the fact that this guy who hardly knew me felt moved by my fate. Also, maybe I knew that, even if I was in the midst of an agonizing wait, commonplace after all for a cancer patient, I was not a lost cause.

I am not able to explain the sudden relief I felt, but Sami's words and body had conveyed certainty. His voice had been tainted by the strange tone provoked by a *truth* that inspires. Even to hear and see that was overwhelming.

We met each other every day after his work.

I was his first lover. Well, almost. Though he'd been around, he remained a tender sweetie—he would let out sighs when I caressed his face. He would whisper, "Yes, yes" and would moan with pleasure as soon as my lips grazed him. He had a wild way of climaxing, with long convulsions crowned by a serious smile, all the while holding his penis like a birth of Venus. Then, pulling the sheets over us, he would nuzzle his head against my stomach. Life hadn't been easy for him either.

I'm not sure who brought me back to life, the prophet or the lover.

Those few weeks of an Indian summer—suddenly it was gorgeous in Paris—constituted our honeymoon. With me, he said, he learned the ropes of love, and he'd turn on the lights after I had turned them off, proclaiming with playful boldness: "I want to see us." He didn't make love to me; it was more of a dance marked with big, abrupt movements. He would puff and pant, and he was blowing out our fear, airing out the Evil, wanting to dig out its roots. Probably, without mentioning them, he was also weeding out and curing secrets. Raking stubbornly to dig up a hidden amulet, he worked diligently at extracting from darkness something we didn't understand. It wasn't love or desire: I felt he was possessed by an amazing need not to seek pleasure but rather to lead us to an orgasm that would be a consolation—perhaps a cure.

Sometimes my worries would come back; he could sense it in the heavy sluggishness that overcame me at those moments. Then he would repeat, almost sententiously:

"Remember the last evening of summer; always remember it."

That had been the evening of his prophecy.

He finally received the offer he was hoping for from the soccer team's management. They were giving him an apartment, a car, a salary, and a cell phone; he would have to live in Barcelona and be constantly available. From then on, the team would be his family. The team's manager told him that players with his potential were a dime a dozen. He had two days to decide whether to accept the offer.

Since he had been a kid, Sami had dreamed about what was happening: a contract with a professional team! It was thanks to me, he affirmed; I had brought him luck.

"You'll come to see me, right? Especially when I invite you to the finals at the Stade de France."

He hugged me and kissed my cheeks, my forehead,

my hands. He also said:

"If you ask me not to, I won't accept; I'll stay with you."

It wasn't the first time he had spoken about living together. It might have been a bit cruel, but I had to explain to him that I remained deeply attached to Benjamin. This time again, I said no. He had to make his life without me. But we would surely remain connected because of his prophecy.

I knew that, even if I had a great tenderness for this guy, I didn't love him enough to give up on the idea of getting back together with Benjamin. I still had to travel through another stage of my journey. By bringing me peace, Sami had restored my need to bring peace to the person who had suffered by my side.

I went with him to the airport when he took off for Barcelona. We kept on staring at each other until he passed through immigration.

Several days before, I had had a follow-up CT scan. He had insisted on staying in Paris until then. He was standing by my side when the radiologist drew near to give me the results. The suspect area remained stable; this meant it must have been scar tissue from the tumor. I was therefore still in remission, and certainly I would be cured. The doctor, a stranger, kept holding my hand in his the whole time he spoke to me.

It was hard to suppress my tears when thanking him.

Sami grabbed me by the shoulders and led me to the hall. There he hugged me and murmured:

"You see? It's over now. It's over."

Sami was right; the end of the journey was near. The only thing left to do was to dock in the strange port where a nonhuman harbor master trumpets: You've reached your destination!

Here I must explain certain technical details.

After you've been diagnosed with cancer, doctors order the installation of a port. This implant makes administering chemotherapy easier and links you to your verdict: It's only removed if remission lasts. At first, the port connects you to the healing process; if it's not taken out, it enters into a contract, a malevolent alliance with the illness, and that which was your road to salvation becomes the road to drowning.

When the time came to take mine out, they sent me to a clinic.

A man was waiting in the corner of the room. Tweed jacket, velvet pants, white shirt, and black loafers. He smiled smugly.

They were going to take me to the operating room imminently. I stripped down and stretched out on my seat, not being very friendly.

"Why are you here?"

I answered curtly. He didn't stop smiling.

"So it's over, if I understand correctly," he said, as if he were talking about a vacation.

I nodded. And with the same tone:

"You are lucky. . . . They are taking yours out; they are putting mine in."

Suddenly, on that lonely stage of indifference where illness propels you, he became closer to me than I could have imagined. Like me, he had understood. He wore the dazed look of those in disbelief to whom the choice of denial has been refused.

A hospital attendant came in and called out my name.

The preoperative and recovery areas were spread out over the same space as the operating room; many gurneys were stationed there. One summer, as a student, I had worked in a similar clinic. I knew what types of things were treated in them: ingrown nails, tonsils, adenoids, phimosis;

ports are installed and circumcisions performed.

Kids were stationed in the back in cribs higher than the nurses, from which tubes dangled. A greenish or bluish light, pale and cold, fell from the ceiling.

A boy was whining; another was frankly crying, yet another screaming frantically. Gowned attendants were worried about having fallen behind schedule. An annoyed nurse, without turning around from the bed where she was installing a drip, ordered one of the boys to shut up. A kid started to call out for his mother. It was contagious. "Can't you make all these kids shut up?" complained an anesthesiologist.

A grandfather and a teenager were waiting like me. Our silence dug an almost tragic well in the midst of so much noise. Nearer to us, we saw a small hand grabbing a bed rail and two enormous eyes filled with silent tears.

Abruptly some gurneys were moved around. It was my turn.

When I returned to the room, the same man was waiting, sitting in the corner, still wearing his civilian clothes.

His turn would not come up until the end of the morning. We would keep each other company. How did it go? I didn't mention the limbo or the innocent kids.

When I had entered the room, I had felt the same annoyance as before and also a vague sense of camaraderie. We hadn't introduced ourselves. Courtesy is almost an incongruous luxury in a hospital. It was weird to shake each other's hands and to say our names. Afterward, we each named our cancer.

He had been given no hope. His lung was shot through with metastases. Six months. He had insisted on trying a chemo regimen, to at least have a chance.

Upon listening to him, I thought that I had a two-year advantage over him. They had given me infinite hope in comparison to him: a one in two chance of being alive five years out. I know, just as he does but does not say it, that doctors are sometimes wrong, miracles do occur, but doctors' prognoses are, most often, correct.

It had been two weeks since his diagnosis. His third child had just been born; his marriage had become stronger after some difficult months.

He asks if he can call his therapist on the phone in front of me. He seems ashamed of having been caught in the act, but what act exactly? He needs a witness. No one can help him now; he knows it, but his old habits die hard: You can tell by the bewildered look carved in his face under the imitation of a smile.

The therapist doesn't pick up.

"Good morning, Doctor, this is Arnaud B. calling. Sorry I haven't called you in a while. My little one is do-ing well, but I've just been hospitalized. In fact, the palpitation problem I had talked to you about seems to be due to lung cancer. I'm being treated at Cochin Hospital. It's rather serious. I'll weather this storm. My wife is with me; we are holding on to each other tight. I wanted you to know; you can call me on my cell phone. Otherwise I'll try calling you back later this afternoon."

He looks at me while talking to himself. He knows I'm a doctor, and he's also talking to me the doctor. He asks me details about the chemo treatments and their effects. Do you get tired? Do you throw up? Can you still make love? He wants so much to make love to his wife. They had been having problems for months, months during which she drove him away. It was partly his fault. Yes, he's not an easy person; yes, he's a workaholic; yes, et cetera, but he did make the effort to go see a therapist... And he doesn't even have a lover! Midlife crisis, maybe? In any case, his wife had also been shaken up; she no longer wants a divorce. It would be stupid now that everything is better. And then, you cannot leave three kids...

The man gets ready for the operating room. He keeps talking about his wife while getting undressed.

"These quibbles are so stupid, aren't they?" he asks.

Wearing only socks and boxers, he paces back and forth.

The paper gown floats around him like a blue Zorro

cape from a Halloween costume. He wants to show me:
He squats down, flexes his biceps, stretches out. He feels
fine! He's not even a little bit out of breath! It's incon-
ceivable. And yet, he saw the X-rays; the lungs are shot
through with metastases. Do I understand? Of course
you do. Stage four! Carcinoid something or other.

"You, you know what that means. And if it's curable.
It must be, at least a little bit."

My silence carries so much power at this point!
I'm paralyzed at the idea of having so much power. To
this stranger, I cannot say with the innocence of a child:
You'll get cured; don't worry about it.

Sporting white socks and burgundy plaid boxers,
he's been catapulted to a place I have never visited. He
cannot understand how it's possible. It's true that you
cannot see anything beyond a certain threshold, especially when a tunnel of certainty forces you to take a single
road leading to your demise.

A nurse comes to inform him that he's the last one on
the schedule for the operating room. Though it's not one
of his character traits, he has learned to become patient.

He asks for my advice, what I did to cope, what I read.
He appeals to God. He speaks again about overworking
during the last few years, his money problems with an as-
sociate. It all seems so trivial, doesn't it? But after this, everything will change; he won't sweat the small stuff.

"You are lucky; you will pull through—I feel it—and begin a new life, right?"

I don't answer and respond with a skeptical smirk. One will get cured; the other won't. And how can I dare tell him that, even in remission, especially in remission, fear never leaves those who know they are condemned?

The nurse comes back with a prescription from the surgeon.

I jot down my telephone number. Upon handing him the paper, I let him know that this is the number not of a doctor but of a friend. Incredulous, he smiles at this last word.

A suffering we hadn't asked for went beyond our understanding and separated us, but also placed us next to each other by chance, every man for himself, an unbearable every man for himself. I waited for him to call. He never did. Nor did I. I was afraid of reeking of good health. I hadn't even blinked when he told me his diagnosis, but I understood his cancer was incurable.

In the last chapter of *If This Is a Man*, Primo Levi describes life in the concentration camp after it's been abandoned by the SS guards. Confined to a barrack with other dying detainees, without heat, electricity or food, he is one of the few to be able to get up and go out to gather scraps in order to survive. His knack for organizing slowly brings back a sense of solidarity. With the help of another comrade, he salvages whatever he can in a camp falling apart. Thanks to his knowledge of chemistry and his pragmatic sense, he is able to build a small alcohol-burning stove, set up electricity using a truck's battery, and improvise a tiny workshop to make candles, which he uses to barter for food with those in other shacks who are in better shape.

At the time, I was again reading my guide. I had even suggested it, wrongly perhaps, to my friend from the clinic. For the peculiar hope one can find in it.

Primo Levi helped me to draw another lesson from my experience. Like any other person thrown into an infernal circle, under a continuous terrorizing threat so commonplace that it becomes part of the self, like any other person trapped in a land of Evil who manages to escape from it, thereafter I held inside of me something infinitely more important than my own ego.

Soon after, I went back to my job at the ER.

As a child and later as a teenager, when at the beginning of the school year they would ask me what I wanted to be later in life, I would always answer with passionate seriousness: a doctor.

Perhaps to simplify things, or maybe to understand a vocation that did not seem to have any roots in my family history, I think of myself as having become a doctor because of my grandmother.

I was still young when she died from this cancer of the lymph nodes, as we used to call it in my home and from which I suffered thirty years later. One of the ironies that fate reserves for certain families.

One day, while we were sitting in a public park—I must have been four or five—I remember telling her:

"Later, I will become a doctor and cure you."

I became a doctor to cure someone who was incurable. I had to become ill myself to imagine the hell she must have gone through before leaving us for good.

The first day I returned to work, I was seized momentarily by panic upon passing in front of a packed waiting room and half-open cubicles. Monitors buzzed and alarms rang out; people shook on gurneys; hazy bluish sensations assaulted me as they had two years before. I wanted to get out of there. Then, as I was heading to the nursing station to meet the night's team, I regained the aplomb of a former medical student: I readjusted my scrubs, buttoned up my coat, and placed a stethoscope around my neck.

Consultation after consultation, the daily routine welcomed me again. I listened, sometimes reassured, giving back a little of what I had received. Through kind words, through conspiring glances and gestures, through my own awkwardness also. I tried hard to fit again in this world where care for others counts as much as care for the self. I healed my soul in the rediscovery of compassion, true compassion—beyond good intentions. Often, by chance, small victories were won—not really over death or loneliness, but victories nonetheless. Scattered glances, intonations, and unspoken words of gratitude, indifference, or frustration effected a revolution in me: People helped me—without knowing it and without my really realizing it—to come to terms with myself; they formed a united front against the abyss that my illness had made me discover and that has haunted me since.

Yet, despite my attentiveness and willingness, the technical dimensions of my work weighed heavily on me as never before: Too rarely did I feel able to give comfort and solace at the level I now demanded of myself. What had opened in me and transformed me was incompatible with the daily practice of medicine with its emphasis on statistics and dehumanized results.

Several weeks after I began to work again, a colleague offered me his place at an emergency medicine conference being held in Zurich.

I didn't go to many of the sessions. I walked on the shore of the lake by which Fritz Zorn had been born, and in the city where he had lived. The ambiance was serene, and I was far from the turmoil I had experienced when I had read *Mars* and that I naturally associated with the city itself. Only the red, piercing eyes of the coots along the Limmat seemed hostile to me: They aimed their laser guns at me but, at the same time, rekindled remnants of the absolute in me. I did not let myself give in to fear: If the coots were vaguely disturbing, the ducks and the gulls were not.

During my short visit, I reread Zorn's story. I felt the need to write again: I had to converse with him again. I was no longer marooned on terrible shores; I could also easily feel true compassion for this man.

Right before going back to work, I had returned to New York to see Benjamin. We were still waiting for each other to open up, but we had decided to restart our transatlantic life.

Benjamin had to spend several days in Paris after I came back from Zurich. When he arrived at the airport, as I reached out to kiss him, he pushed me back. He had caught something that seemed cured, but his doctor hadn't been able to put a finger on the diagnosis.

Assuming my role as doctor and insisting on knowing more, I asked the typical questions about his symptoms and the treatments he had received. He was still worried. I even examined him and played down what was to come. We were now two old brothers who could understand each other.

Seeing him getting undressed, I felt a sad and tender longing for him and, even, a somewhat comical and embarrassing desire. That hadn't happened in a long time.

Several days later, on a beautiful orangey-blue morning, we were waiting in line at an STD clinic.

The wall with peeling paint was adorned with pictures of syphilitic rashes and other delights for lovers of budding illnesses, with statistical graphs, and with posters for disease prevention. Some of the neon lights weren't working. Even in the light, the atmosphere was beige and gray. About ten guys like us were waiting. We were worried, I must admit.

After leaving the consultation cubicle, I found Benjamin leaning forward, gazing intently at the floor. His swollen brown eyelids—like those of a newborn hatchling—gave him a cloistered air like that of Georges de La Tour's *Saint John the Baptist*, whom I had always thought he resembled.

The first time I saw this painting, I had felt an aesthetic emotion—a spiritual sensuality—and a sense of amazement as unexpected as what I had felt during a party at a friend's house when I saw Benjamin for the first time.

In that room bathed by a monochromatic, melancholic light, a grotto of worries and also vague regrets, the Benjamin ingrained in me peeled away from the backdrop of the clinic: a man who didn't know if he could still be loved or if he still was. I could read in his face the detachment of an old soul, attentive and skeptical, perhaps disappointed a priori—the same face that had moved me deeply when I first met him. He was just as before, in the same cocoon.

I went toward him and reassured him: The doctor

was waiting for him; it seemed rather innocuous.

It was in that room, I believe, that we finally escaped from the hell we'd been through.